DS
DS

# THE
# ULTIMATE
# STUDENT
# COOKBOOK

## Cheap, Fun, Easy, Tasty Food

from

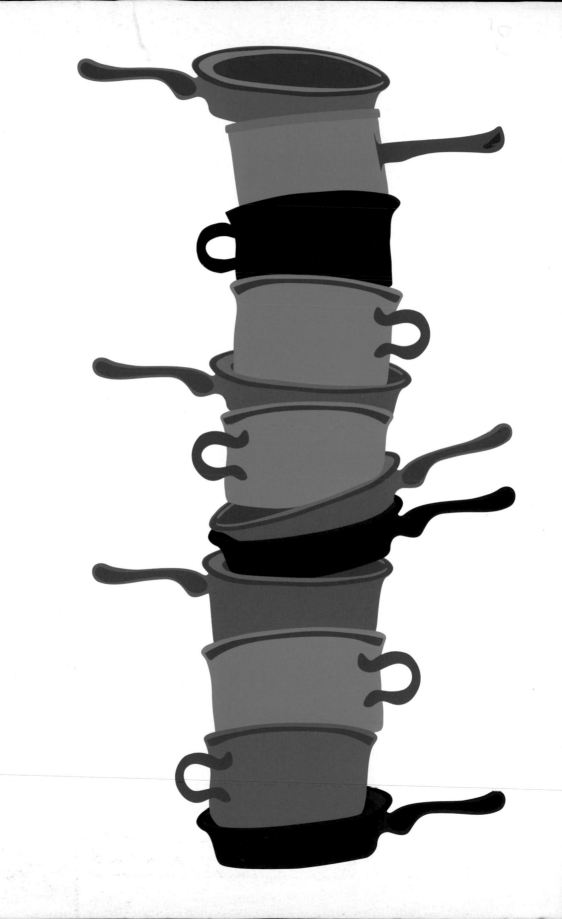

# CONTENTS

Welcome and Introduction      4

Cooking Basics      7

The Building Blocks      25

Quick 'n' Easy      41

Hungry but Penniless      59

Home-cooked Classics      75

Nifty Lunches      109

Crowd Pleasers      127

DIY Takeaways      151

Sweet Stuff      173

Index and Acknowledgements      202

# WELCOME

We are delighted to present to you what we feel is the country's first serious student cookbook.

Combining the knowledge and expertise of studentbeans.com with that of leading recipe technician Rob Allison, we hope we have indeed created the ultimate student cookbook.

Taking our inspiration from the staple student diet of 'beans on toast', studentbeans.com was born in 2005. A few years on, millions of students visit us every month for savings, advice and entertainment – and it is so exciting for us now to have published our very first cookbook. You will be pleased to know that its scope is rather more wide-ranging than 'beans on toast'! As well as revealing new culinary delights, this book will teach you the basics of preparing and eating healthier, tastier food without stretching your budget too far.

Leaving home and being away from our Mum's cooking was a real challenge during our student years. We only wish that there had been something like this around when we were at uni – a clear and simple-to-follow cookbook with properly designed recipes for wholesome and great-tasting food.

In building studentbeans.com, and in all that we do, we have used the idea of 'making life a little more awesome' as a cornerstone. We very much hope that with this book your culinary journey through student life and beyond is a little more awesome too.

*– Michael and James Eder and the team at studentbeans.com*

# INTRODUCTION

There will come a time when the heady first days of new stationery and friends gives way to the realities of university. You are on your own now, left to fend for yourself in among new peers who may seem more prepared and more confident than you. From learning to change your duvet cover to remembering to buy toilet roll, you will pick up new life skills every day. The point of this book is to help you with one of the most daunting: cooking.

From this moment forth, you should regard food as a fun challenge. Shopping, preparing and eating should become an integral part of your life.

Food is so much more than just the fuel that makes our bodies work – it influences everything from our moods to our bank balance, and so should be taken seriously. If you look after your food then it will look after you in so many different ways; be it the familiar taste that cures homesickness, or the delicious chocolate mousse that wins the heart of your future wife or husband. Transforming simple ingredients into meals can be a hugely rewarding endeavour during your time at university and beyond.

We don't want you to be one of those students who grazes on instant noodles and toast because that is the only thing you can prepare without setting the fire alarm off. We want to help you become a student who struts confidently about the kitchen, cooking (and sometimes burning) delicious dishes that will enhance every facet of your university life. So put down the microwave meals and read on to start your culinary journey.

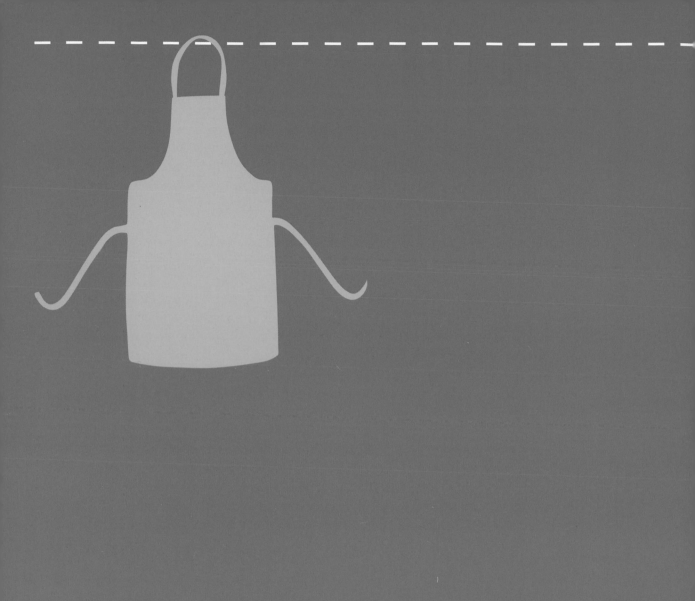

# COOKING BASICS

To every journey there has to be a start, and consider this yours. The following section can be seen as your fresher year – a necessary rite of passage to a higher level of learning. Don't worry though; if you can find your way through the UCAS application system, then cooking should be a breeze.

# MEASUREMENTS

Cooking is very much about the senses: smelling, seeing, feeling and tasting. Getting the hang of all this is something that is developed over time, so you will get there eventually, it just takes practice. Throughout the book we've used more or less accurate measures, and that's because generally you will need to know how much of an ingredient to include for it to succeed. Follow the guidelines in this book for quantities as best you can, but it won't matter if you use a large onion rather than a medium onion. To make things a bit easier, we have given you a breakdown of estimate measures, just in case your student digs doesn't have a set of scales.

## 1 MUG (350ML)

| | |
|---|---|
| rice | 260g |
| sugar (caster or granulated) | 310g |
| grated Cheddar cheese | 150g |
| frozen peas | 150g |
| flour | 200g |
| dried breadcrumbs | 150g |
| puy lentils | 250g |
| dried macaroni | 210g |
| dried fusilli | 150g |
| bulgur wheat | 270g |
| Brussels sprouts | 120g |
| raspberries | 180g |
| quinoa | 270g |
| raisins | 240g |
| frozen berries | 230g |
| grated Parmesan cheese | 150g |
| chopped nuts | 170g |
| mixed whole nuts | 200g |

## ½ MUG (175ML)

| | |
|---|---|
| rice | 130g |
| sugar (caster or granulated) | 165g |
| grated Cheddar cheese | 75g |
| frozen peas | 75g |
| flour | 100g |
| dried breadcrumbs | 75g |
| puy lentils | 125g |
| dried macaroni | 105g |
| dried fusilli | 75g |
| bulgur wheat | 135g |
| Brussels sprouts | 60g |
| raspberries | 90g |
| quinoa | 135g |
| raisins | 120g |
| frozen berries | 115g |
| grated Parmesan cheese | 75g |
| chopped nuts | 85g |
| mixed whole nuts | 200g |

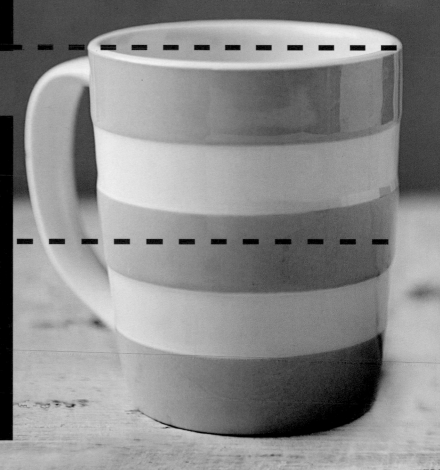

**1 PINT (568ML)**

| | |
|---|---|
| rice | 420g |
| sugar (caster or granulated) | 500g |
| grated Cheddar cheese | 240g |
| frozen peas | 250g |
| flour | 330g |
| dried breadcrumbs | 250g |
| puy lentils | 410g |
| dried macaroni | 340g |
| dried fusilli | 250g |
| bulgur wheat | 440g |
| Brussels sprouts | 200g |
| raspberries | 300g |
| quinoa | 430g |
| raisins | 390g |
| frozen berries | 370g |
| grated Parmesan cheese | 240g |
| chopped nuts | 280g |
| mixed whole nuts | 320g |

**½ PINT (284ML)**

| | |
|---|---|
| rice | 210g |
| sugar (caster or granulated) | 250g |
| grated Cheddar cheese | 120g |
| frozen peas | 125g |
| flour | 165g |
| dried breadcrumbs | 125g |
| puy lentils | 205g |
| dried macaroni | 170g |
| dried fusilli | 125g |
| bulgur wheat | 220g |
| Brussels sprout | 100g |
| raspberries | 150g |
| quinoa | 215g |
| raisins | 195g |
| frozen berries | 185g |
| grated Parmesan cheese | 120g |
| chopped nuts | 140g |
| mixed whole nuts | 160g |

# KITCHEN KIT

We don't expect you to blow your first loan cheque on the finest forged Japanese knives or professional chef equipment, but it is worthwhile investing in the right items. If looked after properly, they will see you through to the end of your course and beyond.

Below is a breakdown of the basic kitchen kit you will need to cook the meals in this book.

## KNIVES

You will need two knives – one main chopper, plus a smaller knife for completing the more fiddly cutting tasks. One word of warning: once you've bought your knives, hoard them. Lending them out will quicken the blunting process, because everybody chops in a different way.

## WOODEN CHOPPING BOARD

Plastic boards may seem like a bargain choice, but the grooves developed from cutting can collect moisture, resulting in gross fungal growth. Because wood is breathable, it's a safer and more hygienic option.

## OVENPROOF DISH

Either a ceramic or cast-iron ovenproof dish in which you can roast chicken as well as make a lasagne. Although cast iron is better, they can be expensive, but they are often discounted in sales and will last a lifetime. Size-wise, go for one around 28 x 15cm. A number of the recipes in this book were tested in a dish this size, so you know that it will be money well spent.

## FRYING PAN AND SAUCEPAN

Try to buy the best non-stick pans you can afford – the investment will be worth it. Look after them and avoid scratching them with metal implements or putting them in a dishwasher where the coating will slowly be worn off by the abrasive salts. As far as size goes, a 20–25cm wide frying pan that has an ovenproof handle and a saucepan (that comes with a lid) with a capacity of more than 1.5 litres are the most versatile options.

## MISCELLANEOUS ITEMS

Try to convince your mum that it's time for her to update her equipment and then sneak the following into your bag:

Mixing bowl

Scales*

Tin opener

Measuring jug

Potato masher

Colander and/or sieve

Wooden spoon

Box grater

Vegetable peeler

Whisk

Pair of tongs

Spatula

Baking tray or sheet

Muffin tin

Cake and/or loaf tin

*Refer to our measuring guide on pages 8–9 if you don't have scales handy.*

# STORECUPBOARD AND FRIDGE STANDBYS

It is highly likely that when your parents first drop you off at university they will pay for your first big shop. This is your chance to stock up, so make the most of it. The following should definitely make it into your basket, as they will form the basis of your storecupboard and you'll then only need a handful of fresh ingredients to be on your way to making a delicious meal.

## ESSENTIALS

- Vegetable oil and light olive oil
- Salt
- Black pepper
- Tinned tomatoes
- Butter
- Milk
- Cheddar cheese
- Chicken stock (cubes or powder)
- Light soy sauce
- Plain flour
- Pasta – spaghetti plus one other shape (e.g. fusilli)
- Rice
- Bread
- Eggs
- Onions

## SHOPPING AND PLANNING

When you leave home, not only will you lose your parents' bank balance, but also their mode of transport. The large supermarkets that offer the best range of produce at the best value are often located far from campus, so it is a good idea to **limit your trips to once a week.** To make the most of this weekly shop it is vital that you **buy in bulk** and do a bit of planning. Work out what you will eat that week and **buy only those ingredients that you need.** We are not naïve enough to think that things always go as planned – all too often a group tutorial will evolve into a drinking session capped with a takeaway – but you can always put that minced beef you were planning on cooking in the freezer or cook it another day. If you start with the right intentions, your life will become easier and cheaper.

Bear in mind that all of the meals in the planner (see opposite page) are for more than one person, and that we have assumed the price of whole packets of items such as spaghetti and butter, which will last into the next week. The example shopping list on the opposite page will come to a total of about £35–£40, depending on where you shop and what deals are on offer. Of course, if this is beyond your weekly budget, adjust the weekly planner and shopping list as needed by simplifying your meals.

# WEEKLY FOOD PLANNER (EXAMPLE)

|  | MONDAY | TUESDAY | WEDNESDAY | THURSDAY | FRIDAY | SATURDAY | SUNDAY |
|---|---|---|---|---|---|---|---|
| **BREAKFAST** | Cereal | Cereal | Toast | Fry-up | Croissant | Too hungover to eat | Sweetcorn Fritters (see page 54) |
| **LUNCH** | Leftover chicken sandwich | Tomatoes on Toast (see page 60) | Multi-purpose Mince (see page 38) | No food needed | Salad | Cheese and Ham Toastie (see page 52) | Roast Chicken (see page 96) |
| **DINNER** | Multi-purpose Mince (see page 38) | Eggs Pipérade (see page 50) | Takeaway | Chicken Dinner in a Tray (see page 78) | Sausage and Tomato Spaghetti (see page 68) | Friend's place for dinner | Boiled egg, if anything |

**SHOPPING LIST**

800g cherry tomatoes

1 avocado

1 lime

2 spring onions

2 red onions

2 red peppers

Fresh thyme

Fresh rosemary

4 potatoes

200g tenderstem broccoli

2 carrots

1 onion

1 heart of celery

1 bulb of garlic

1 red chilli

Butter

Cereal

Croissants

Loaf of bread

6 eggs

Tomato purée

Dried bay leaves

Dried oregano

Beef stock cubes

2 x 400g tins of chopped tomatoes

1 x 250g pack of Cheddar cheese

1 x pack of sliced ham

1 x 200g tin of sweetcorn

6 chicken thighs

1 whole chicken

1 x 500g pack of minced beef

# EATING WELL DURING EXAM TIME AND BEYOND

It is tempting for anyone who has left home to exist on pizza, kebabs and lager alone. As fun as this may be, it will soon leave you with gout, diabetes or at least an acne-ridden face and a rapidly expanding waistline – not cool. During busy times it might be tempting to just give up on preparing and eating proper meals, substituting them for a trip to the takeaway. Try instead to consider the time spent cooking yourself a healthy meal as the perfect time to de-stress; concentrate on the cooking and preparation, leaving all your exam worries at the kitchen door.

We will not presume to take the place of your mum and nag you to eat more fruit and vegetables, but do try; they help your brain and improve energy levels. It is worth considering the following when choosing what to cook:

Colour is an excellent guide to a healthy diet. The more colourful the food on your plate, the better it is for you. Try to add greens (spinach, cabbage, pak choi) and reds (beetroot, tomatoes) to your plate – not only will they add nutrients, but they will taste good.

Processed foods like ready meals really are the foodstuff of the devil. Try not to eat more than one a week, if any.

Consider the idea of going vegetarian for a day. Not only is it good for your body, and the environment, but it is also excellent for your bank balance.

Try to eat a range of food groups. Too many carbs and you'll feel sluggish, too much meat and you'll need a colonic. A little of everything does you good.

# SURVIVAL SKILLS

Food is a perishable good that has to be dealt with properly. From storage to reheating, if you follow some very basic principles you will avoid poisoning yourself and wasting perfectly good food.

 Plan ahead and cook more food than you need so that leftovers can be enjoyed the next day or frozen for another time.

 Freeze in small portions so that you don't have to defrost your entire stock at once.

 Allow hot food to cool completely before covering and transferring to the fridge or freezer.

 When reheating (especially meat) make sure it is brought to a high temperature (above 75°C) for at least 2 minutes.

 DON'T refreeze defrosted food.

 Trust your senses – don't cook or eat something if it smells or looks bad. Chances are, if it smells bad, and it looks bad, it probably is bad.

# SIMPLE SALAD DRESSINGS

Salads are an excellent way to get your five a day and they are super-easy to throw together. Even the smallest supermarkets stock a good range of leaves, all picked and pre-washed. There are very few things nicer to eat on a hot summer's day than a piece of grilled meat and a handful of fresh salad leaves dressed simply with a little olive oil and lemon juice. But if you want something a little different, then try one of the following dressings.

**CLASSIC FRENCH**
- Mix 1 teaspoon of Dijon mustard,
- 2 teaspoons of white wine vinegar and
- 5 tablespoons of olive oil until you have
- a smooth dressing.

**CHEAT'S CAESAR**
- Chop 5 anchovy fillets as finely as you
- can and place them in a bowl along with
- 3 heaped tablespoons of mayonnaise,
- 1 tablespoon each of white wine vinegar
- and grated Parmesan cheese and enough
- water to mix to a pouring consistency.

**ASIAN DRESSING**
- Pour 1 tablespoon of fish sauce, the juice of
- 3 limes, 1 teaspoon of sugar and a drizzle
- of sesame oil into a bowl and mix well
- to combine. Pour over shredded fennel,
- carrots and cucumber for a deliciously
- different salad that goes perfectly with fish.

# EAT YOUR VEG

Vegetables are your basic, vibrant, vitamin-filled ingredients that the Government and your well-meaning parents keep blabbing on at you to eat. They have a point though. You should try to make a habit of always having some sort of vegetable with at least one meal of the day. Throughout the book there are some delectable vegetable dishes you can try, but one indispensable cooking skill is to know how to boil your vegetables to serve as a side dish.

As a general rule of thumb, prepared vegetables should be dropped into a generous amount of boiling water, which has had 2 teaspoons of salt added. To state the obvious, water is boiling when heated to a point when there are lots of bubbles emerging on the surface. The below table shows you everything you need to know about boiled veg.

| | PREPARATION | AMOUNT (MUG) | SERVINGS | COOKING TIME (MINS) |
|---|---|---|---|---|
| BROCCOLI | Trim the florets from the stalk. Discard the stalk | 1 | 2 | 4 |
| FINE BEANS | Cut off the stalk end | 1 – standing in mug | 2 | 3 |
| FROZEN PEAS | – | 1 | 2 | 3 |
| ASPARAGUS | Hold at each end and bend until it snaps. Only use the end with the pretty top | 1 – spears standing in mug | 2 | 4 |
| MANGETOUT | | 1 – standing in mug | 2 | 3 |
| SAVOY CABBAGE | Outer leaves removed. Stalk in the middle removed, shredded into 1cm pieces | 2 | 2 | 3 |
| CARROTS | Peeled, and sliced into 1cm rounds | 1 | 2 | 5 |
| POTATOES | Peel and wash before chopping into 3cm chunks | 2 | 2 | 8 |

# IDEAS WITH VEG

## SPINACH

Often already conveniently picked and packaged in almost every supermarket, spinach truly is the perfect accompaniment to anything from steak to grilled fish.

- Heat a small knob of butter in a large frying pan until melted and bubbling. Add 2 large handfuls of spinach per person and wilt, while stirring, for a few seconds. Season and serve.

- Spinach can easily be added at the very end of cooking a variety of dishes. Try it stirred into instant noodles to add a healthy green streak.

## CABBAGE

You can simply boil up cabbage for it to be a delicious side, but there are a couple more interesting ways to prepare it if you are feeling adventurous:

### WHITE CABBAGE COLESLAW

Remove the woody core of half a white cabbage and shred the leaves as finely as you can. Put in a bowl along with 2 peeled and grated carrots, ½ a peeled and grated red onion, salt and pepper and 6 heaped tablespoons of mayonnaise to create a delicious coleslaw to go with any grilled or barbecued meat.

### SAVOY CABBAGE AND BACON

Heat a large knob of butter in a saucepan over a high heat. When melted and bubbling, add 2 rashers of chopped smoked streaky bacon and fry for 3 minutes until cooked and a little golden. Add half a shredded savoy cabbage along with 100ml of chicken stock. Place a lid on top, reduce the heat to medium and cook for about 6 minutes until the cabbage is just tender.

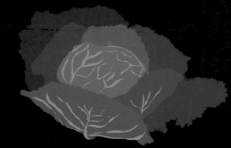

Humble in stature, bland in looks, but peerless in terms of versatility, dependability and ease of use, the potato is God's gift to studentkind. They also sit quite merrily in that awkward gap between the toaster and fridge for at least a week without even a breath of refrigeration. You can't get more low maintenance than that.

Here are the best ways to cook spuds:

## MASHED

Add 2 peeled, washed and evenly diced potatoes per person to a saucepan of boiling water. Make sure the potatoes are well submerged in the water. Boil for 12–15 minutes until very tender. Drain through a colander and leave to stand while you heat up 2 large knobs of butter and a splash of milk in the still-warm saucepan. Tip the cooked potatoes in and mash until all lumps are eradicated. Season generously with salt and pepper.

## BAKED

Preheat your oven to 190°C (gas mark 5). Wash and dry 1 potato per person. Stab your potato with a fork in at least two places before placing in the oven for just over an hour. If you are in a hurry, then blast your washed and pricked potato in the microwave for 6 minutes before finishing in the oven for 30 minutes.

## ROASTED

Pour 3 tablespoons of oil into a baking tray and place in an oven preheated to 200°C (gas mark 6) for 8 minutes. Peel 1 ½ potatoes per person and chop into rough 5cm square pieces. Drop the chopped potatoes into boiling water and boil for 8–10 minutes until they are almost cooked through. Drain in a colander and waft a couple of times to release excess steam.

Tumble the potatoes back into the saucepan, put the lid on top and give them a good shake to rough up the edges. Carefully remove your hot tray from the oven and tip the potatoes into the oil. Place the potatoes back in the oven and roast for about 45 minutes, turning a couple of times to ensure even browning. Season before serving.

## WEDGES

Drizzle a roasting tray with oil and place in an oven preheated to 190°C (gas mark 5) for 5 minutes. Wash and pat dry 1 potato per person. Slice the potato in half lengthways, before splitting each half into 3 wedges. Remove your roasting tray from the oven and carefully tumble your potato wedges into the hot oil. Place the tray back in the oven and roast for 45 minutes, turning a couple of times. Season well and serve.

**Tip:** *Don't forget that sweet potatoes are just a sweeter and healthier version of normal potatoes. Although they cannot be directly substituted into all the above methods, they do make the most delicious wedges.*

**4** SLICE 'N' DICE

**5**

**6**

1. Sliced garlic
2. Diced carrot
3. Sliced red onion
4. Diced white onion
5. Sliced celery
6. Diced garlic

# RICE AND PASTA

**These will become the mainstay of your university meals, for two very good reasons: they are cheap and filling. It is therefore very important that you know how to cook them.**

**Both rice and pasta come in wholemeal or white varieties. The white versions are what you are most likely already familiar with, however it is worth trying out the wholemeal varieties as they are much better for you. Without going into in-depth dietary science, they basically make you feel less bloated and sluggish. If you only eat wholemeal pasta and rice for a short period in your university career then make it exam time; the slower-releasing carbs will ensure your body and mind are in the best state possible for those all-important finals.**

## HOW TO COOK RICE

There are two kinds of rice that require different cooking methods. Long-grain, easy-cook rice is simply added to a generous amount of boiling water and drained when cooked. It really is almost impossible to get wrong. Having said this, it is also the worst kind of rice in terms of flavour.

The best type of rice is either basmati or jasmine, cooked using what is called the 'absorption method'. No, we haven't stolen the term from a chemistry textbook; this is a real cookery method, and this is how you do it to get two portions of perfectly cooked rice:

- **Pour** 1 x mug of rice into a saucepan that has a lid. Pour in enough water to cover. If you have time, leave the rice to soak for 15 minutes.

- **Carefully** pour out as much of the soaking water as possible. Using the same mug used to measure the rice with, pour in 1 ½ mugs of fresh water.

- **Place** the saucepan over a high heat and bring to the boil. Once the water is boiling rapidly, place the lid on top and reduce the heat to the lowest possible setting. Leave the rice to cook like this for 6 minutes. Turn off the heat and allow to sit (with the lid on) for a further 5 minutes, after which you will have perfect rice.

# HOW TO COOK PASTA

There are enough shapes and sizes of pasta to eat a different one every day. In the pasta recipes that follow we've told you what pasta shape to use for any given dish, but you don't need to stick to it. As for quantities, use the spaghetti guide to the right and the rough breakdown of measurements on pages 8–9. Basically, ½ pint or 1 mug of dried pasta shapes will be more than enough per person. All shop-bought pasta will come with cooking instructions for you to follow, but we also offer the following tips:

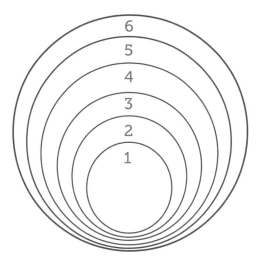

Spaghetti measure

- Timings on the packet can vary, so check for doneness a minute or so before the allocated time is up, and check again just before draining.

- Cook pasta in loads of simmering water with a teaspoon of salt added to it.

- Once your pasta is cooked, season it with a drizzle of olive oil and salt and pepper.

- If you cook too much pasta, leave it to cool completely, cover and refrigerate. To reheat simply immerse in boiling water for 2 minutes.

# HOW TO USE THIS BOOK

**The recipes in this book feature little symbols that we have used to highlight a certain special something. Here are the symbols decoded:**

 brain food, ideal for when you are cramming in study for that all-important exam

 suitable for vegetarians

 wow-factor dishes. These will impress in flavour and presentation for when you want to wow your friends and family

 hangover-busting dishes, for those tough times we all know too well . . .

 less than £1.50* per person

 between £1.50–£2.50* per person

 between £2.50–£3.50* per person

* Estimates are based on an average of supermarket prices at the time of writing and excluding storecupboard essentials.

# THE BUILDING BLOCKS

The recipes that follow will hopefully become the building blocks for your culinary temple. They are the basic recipes that have a multitude of uses. As you cook them, you will develop your cooking 'DNA', making it easier to cook other dishes.

Even if you choose to delve straight into the recipes further on in the book, try to refer to this chapter once in a while. The recipes will help you in the long run.

# ANY WHICH WAY WITH EGGS

We do not know who first thought to crack open the egg from a chicken and begin experimenting with it, but what we do know is that we owe them a huge debt of gratitude. Over the years, eggs have become essential to all areas of cookery. We want you to tap into this magical foodstuff, so below are key methods of cooking eggs, which are too often overlooked by other cookbooks as too simple to include. Well, not by us. We think the simpler the better. All of the following recipes will serve one.

## BOILED EGG

1 **egg**

**Salt** and **pepper**

**Fill** a small pan two-thirds of the way up with water and bring to the boil.

**Lower** the egg into the pan carefully.

**Simmer** for 5 minutes for a rich, runny yolk and 10–12 minutes for a hard-boiled egg you can slice up. Season with salt and pepper and serve.

## SCRAMBLED EGG

There is only one secret to sublime scrambled eggs and that is using lots of butter. Get ready for the creamiest and most delicious plate of eggs you could wish for.

2 **eggs**

Generous knob of **butter**

1 slice of **buttered toast**

**Salt** and **pepper**

**Crack** the eggs into a bowl, season generously, then use a fork to whisk together well.

**Heat** the butter in a saucepan over a medium heat. Once melted and bubbling, pour in the whisked eggs.

**Stir** the eggs almost constantly as they begin to come together – this should take about 4–5 minutes. The secret is to turn the heat off when the eggs still look a little liquid. Once the heat is off, continue to stir the eggs and the residual heat will finish off the cooking.

**Now** spoon your incredibly creamy scrambled eggs over hot toast, top with a little extra black pepper and get stuck in.

# FRIED EGG

Everybody should know how to fry an egg. The knowledge should somehow be passed from mother to child via the umbilical cord. However, it's not. So it's down to us to give you our version.

2 tbsp **oil**

1 **egg**

1 slice of **buttered toast**

**Heat** the oil in a frying pan over a medium to high heat. Once hot, crack the egg into the pan. Do not crack it from any great height as you may well break the yolk.

**Cook** the egg for 2 minutes until the white has set.

**Take** a teaspoon and begin gently scooping up some of the hot oil and spooning it over the yolk. Repeat this process a few times and you will see that the raw white on the surface of the yolk is beginning to turn opaque – this means that it is cooked.

**This** process should take you about 1 minute. By this time your egg is perfectly fried and ready to top your slice of buttered toast.

# POACHED EGG

One of the healthiest and most delicious ways to prepare an egg is to poach it.

1 **egg**

1 slice of **buttered toast**

**Salt** and **pepper**

**Tip:** *For a delicious breakfast, cook the poached egg as instructed, but use it to top a toasted English muffin, add some wilted spinach and a little shop-bought hollandaise sauce.*

**Fill** a large saucepan with water and heat it over a medium to high heat until it is just below boiling point – there should be a few small bubbles shooting from the bottom of the pan to the surface.

**Crack** your egg into a mug or a bowl (this will help the egg retain its shape), and when the water is hot gently slide your egg in. Leave the egg to cook on the low temperature for 3–4 minutes. If the water begins to boil too hard, reduce the heat to maintain a gentle simmer.

**The** egg is cooked when the yolk is masked by a thin layer of cooked, fully-formed white, but it will still be soft to the touch. Remove the poached egg with a slotted spoon and place onto hot buttered toast.

**Season** with salt and pepper, dig in and marvel at the velvety richness of your perfectly poached egg.

# SIMPLE TOMATO SAUCE

Once you've cooked this sauce and realised quite how easy it is, you will soon find that pre-prepared jarred sauces are but a distant, expensive and not very tasty memory.

**MAKES 500G**

2 tbsp **olive oil**

1 **onion**, peeled and finely chopped

1 **garlic** clove, peeled and finely chopped

1 x 400g tin of **chopped tomatoes**

1 tsp **sugar**

Bunch of fresh **basil**, leaves only, roughly ripped

**Salt** and **pepper**

**Heat** the oil in a saucepan over a medium to high heat. Add the chopped onion and fry for 5 minutes while stirring regularly. Add the garlic and continue to fry and stir for another 3 minutes. Add the tinned chopped tomatoes, sugar, basil and a little salt and pepper.

**Reduce** the heat to medium to low and leave the mixture to simmer for 12–15 minutes. By this point it should have thickened. Taste one more time and add more salt and pepper if needed.

**Tip:** *This sauce freezes very well, so it is worth cooking in big batches.*

# WHITE SAUCE

These days, some versions of white sauce try to cram in so many ingredients that are simply not needed, such as 'stabilisers' and 'emulsifiers'. Here's how to prepare it the way people have managed for centuries without those magical non-ingredients. Learning how to cook this recipe is your first key to unlocking large swathes of cooking. From this sauce you can make all manner of dishes, from cauliflower cheese to soufflés.

**MAKES 800G
(enough to make a
lasagne)**

Large **knob** of butter
(about 75g)

5 tbsp **plain flour**

600ml **milk**

**Melt** the butter in a saucepan over a medium to high heat. Once it has melted, add the flour and stir well with a wooden spoon until the ingredients are well incorporated into a roux. Cook the mixture, stirring almost constantly, for 2 minutes.

**Take** the saucepan off the heat, pour in a quarter of the milk and stir well until it has mixed in with the butter and flour mix. Add another quarter of the milk and again stir to combine. The mixture should start to become looser now. Add a third quarter of milk and mix again before placing the pan back over the heat. Pour in the remaining milk and continue stirring with a wooden spoon until the mixture comes up to boiling point.

**Reduce** the temperature to a simmer and cook, stirring, for 2–3 minutes. The sauce should become thicker. Voila! Your first white sauce made, and not a jar in sight.

**Variation:** *To make this into a cheese sauce is incredibly simple. Just beat in 100g grated Cheddar and 25g grated Parmesan a little at a time once the sauce has thickened.*

**Tips:** *If your white sauce hasn't thickened, then continue cooking the sauce for a little longer. Be careful and keep a close eye on the sauce because if you find that it has overcooked and burnt you will need to start afresh.*

# SODA BREAD

Bread does not always have to be made from a mixture of yeast and elbow grease; there is a much simpler method. If you can't get hold of buttermilk, then stir ½ teaspoon of lemon juice into 300ml of milk and leave it to stand for 5 minutes before using.

**SERVES 4**

350g **plain flour**, plus
a little extra
for dusting
1½ tsp **bicarbonate
of soda**
1 tsp **salt**
300ml **buttermilk**

**Preheat** the oven to 200°C (gas mark 6).

**Put** the flour, bicarbonate of soda and salt in a large bowl. Pour in half of the buttermilk and mix with a spoon. Now add the remaining buttermilk and get your hands in the bowl to mix thoroughly until you are left with a thick dough.

**Lightly** flour a baking tray and plonk the dough straight onto it. Roughly create a round shape with your hands, and with a knife cut a deep cross into the top, about a quarter of the way into the dough, to create the traditional shape.

**Bake** in the preheated oven for 35 minutes until the outside is nicely browned. To check if the bread is cooked all the way through, simply give the base a couple of quick taps. If it sounds hollow, your bread is ready.

**Serve** warm from the oven with a little butter.

**Variations**: *This recipe is so easy to expand upon – the variations are only limited by your imagination. Once you have cooked it a couple of times and are happy with how it works, try adding other flavourings, such as cooked bacon, Cheddar cheese or roughly chopped walnuts.*

# BASIC PANCAKES

Why wait until Shrove Tuesday to cook pancakes? When something so delicious can be made from such humble and easy-to-procure ingredients it is a surprise that every day isn't pancake day.

**MAKES 12**

200g **plain flour**

3 **eggs**, beaten

250ml **milk**

100ml **water**

Generous knob of **butter,** melted, plus a little extra for frying

**Tip** the flour into a large mixing bowl and make a small well in the middle. Pour in the eggs and use a wooden spoon to begin lightly beating the flour into the eggs.

**Pour** in half of the milk and water mixture and lightly beat again, working in a little more flour before pouring in the remaining milk and water and beating thoroughly until you are left with a smooth and runny batter. Add the melted butter and mix. It is now a good idea to transfer your batter to a measuring jug to make it easier to pour.

**Heat** a good non-stick frying pan over a high heat and add a little cube of butter. Once it has melted, pour some of the batter mixture into the pan and swirl it around to cover the base. Let the pancake fry for 1 minute before flipping it with a dextrous flick of the wrist – or with the help of a spatula. Continue to fry for a further minute before carefully sliding onto a plate and repeating until the remaining batter is used up.

**Ideas** for toppings really are endless – good old-fashioned sugar and lemon juice, maple syrup, golden syrup, chocolate spread, jam . . .

# GNOCCHI

Gnocchi is a great alternative to pasta — it's unbelievably versatile and can be used as a delicious vehicle for many flavours and sauces, from a jar of shop-bought pesto to simple tomato sauce (see page 29). Although you can buy pre-prepared gnocchi, we think that there is no better way to procrastinate on doing revision than pouring yourself a glass of wine and preparing some fresh gnocchi. Once you learn the basic recipe below, you'll be experimenting with flavours in no time.

**SERVES 4**

750g floury **potatoes**, such as Maris Piper or King Edwards

175g **plain flour**, plus a little extra for dusting

2 **egg yolks**

**Olive oil**, to drizzle

**Salt** and **pepper**

**Peel** the potatoes and chop them into reasonably big pieces. Bring a large saucepan of salted water to boiling point, tip in the chopped potatoes and cook for about 15–20 minutes or until they are soft all the way through. Use a colander to drain the potatoes, then leave to stand for 3–4 minutes so some of the moisture evaporates.

**Mash** the potatoes as smoothly as possible. You can give them an extra going over with a whisk, too, which will get them extra smooth.

**Tip** in the flour and the egg yolks. Work them in either with a wooden spoon or preferably your hands. You should be left with quite a firm dough. Tip the dough out onto a floured surface and split into 8 equal portions.

**Take** each portion of dough in turn and use your hands to roll into a long sausage shape, about as thick as your finger, on the floured surface. Chop the sausage shape at roughly 1 ½ cm intervals to create your olive-sized gnocchi. Gently roll the pieces over the back of a fork to get that traditional grooved effect. Repeat the process with the remaining dough.

**Bring** a large saucepan of salted water to boiling point, then tip in the gnocchi. They only need 2–3 minutes to cook through. You can tell when they are cooked as they tend to rise to the surface. Drain the gnocchi and season with olive oil, salt and pepper.

**Variation:** *What we didn't tell you is that the recipe we have given you for gnocchi can also be used to make classic Irish potato cakes. All you have to do is divide your dough into 6 and mould into rough cake shapes between your palms. Fry them in a mixture of 2 tablespoons of oil and 2 tablespoons of butter for about 3 minutes per side,* et voila! *Perfect potato cakes ready to be served alongside baked beans, fried eggs and sausages for a hangover-busting breakfast.*

# MULTI-PURPOSE MINCE

This recipe requires a little more effort than your standard 'jar of tomato sauce' method, but we guarantee it is more than worth it. We would go so far as to say that this dish should become a weekly ritual, as embedded in the student psyche as Wednesday-night socials. It is packed full of goodness, can be frozen and is as versatile as a Swiss army knife (see Variations).

## SERVES 6

4 tbsp **olive oil**

1 **onion**, peeled and finely chopped

2 **garlic** cloves, peeled and finely chopped

2 **carrots**, peeled and finely chopped

3 **celery** sticks, finely chopped

500g **minced beef**

2 tbsp **tomato purée**

2 sprigs **fresh thyme**

3 dried **bay leaves**

1 glass of **red wine** (optional)

1 x 400g tin of **chopped tomatoes**

500ml **beef** or **vegetable stock**

**Salt** and **pepper**

**Heat** half the oil in a large saucepan over a medium to high heat. Once hot, add the onion, garlic, carrots and celery. Cook this for about 10 minutes, stirring periodically to avoid burning.

**While** the vegetables are cooking, heat the remaining oil in a large frying pan over a very high heat. Once the oil has begun to smoke, add half of the minced beef. You are aiming to brown the meat and break it up. This should take 3–4 minutes. Try and move the mince around as little as possible; this will help keep the heat in the pan and brown the meat more effectively. Once the meat is brown, tip it straight into the pan with the cooking vegetables and stir to combine. Place the frying pan back on the hob and repeat the browning process with the remaining mince.

**You** should now have a large saucepan over a medium to high heat with cooked vegetables and browned mince. Stir everything well to combine and season with salt and a generous amount of black pepper. Turn up the heat to maximum.

**Add** the tomato purée, thyme sprigs and bay leaves. Fry the mixture for 2–3 minutes, stirring regularly to avoid sticking and burning. Pour in the red wine (if using) – it should almost instantly boil and begin to reduce. Continue to boil the red wine for 2 minutes to cook out the raw alcohol flavour. Tip in the tin of tomatoes and add the stock. Bring the mixture to the boil, then reduce the heat to low and simmer uncovered.

**For** the impatient among you, this basic Bolognese sauce is edible after 10 minutes of simmering. However, this dish is best simmered for a minimum of 1 ½ hours, topping up every now and then with a little water when needed so that it doesn't dry out and burn on the bottom of the pan. The Bolognese only becomes richer with extended cooking and can be kept simmering for up to 3 hours. After this time the flavours will have intensified and the meat will have been broken down to its most meltingly delicious.

**This** is your go-to everything sauce: it can be lathered over pasta, used as a shepherd's pie base or as your basic Bolognese sauce – once you've tried it, you'll soon be uttering those beautiful words, 'Dolmio who?'

**Variations:** *Use it for basic spag bol; layer with pasta sheets and white sauce to make the ultimate lasagne (see page 148); add a can of beans and a handful of spinach to make a quick dinner; spoon onto slices of bread and scoff in a drunken frenzy, and even set between bricks to build a house.*

**Tip:** *Make the entire recipe and then separate the leftovers into individual portions before freezing. It defrosts very well from frozen in the microwave, which means you will always have a quick, easy and satisfying meal on hand.*

# QUICK 'N' EASY

Whether it's because of lectures or your social life, there are times at university when it feels like you're juggling lots of plates. Too often at these moments it is easy to dive into the depths of the deep freezer and pull out a meal to bung in the microwave; an unsatisfying meal that burns the roof of your mouth as your delve in before it has had time enough to cool.

Instead, we suggest that you cook one of our following quick fixes. Every recipe in this chapter can be cooked in less than 20 minutes, and is delicious. Many can be prepared in less than 10 minutes, if you have your wits about you. As well as being quick, they are generally well-balanced recipes, so instead of that lingering guilt and bloatedness that often comes after eating a processed meal, you will feel virtuous and light on your feet.  What more could you ask for?

# BROCCOLI AND ANCHOVY SPAGHETTI

This dish is all about the wondrous combination of its ingredients. Nothing brings out the beautifully subtle flavour of broccoli more than anchovies. Boosted by a sprinkling of rosemary and set alight with a little red chilli, it is no wonder this combination is a speedy classic.

## SERVES 2

**Spaghetti** to serve 2 (see page 23)

½ head of **broccoli**, florets only

4 tbsp **olive oil**

1 **garlic** clove, peeled and finely sliced

6 **anchovy fillets** from a tin, drained and finely chopped

1 **red chilli**, finely sliced (deseeded if you don't like it too hot)

1 fresh **rosemary** sprig, leaves only, finely chopped

**Salt** and **pepper**

**Bring** a large saucepan of salted water to the boil. Once boiling, add your dried spaghetti, encouraging it to slide into the water, and cook according to the packet instructions – it should take about 8–10 minutes. When the pasta is about 3 minutes from being cooked, add the broccoli florets to the pan. Once cooked, drain the pasta and the broccoli and leave to rest in the colander.

**Meanwhile**, heat the oil in a frying pan set over a medium heat. Add the garlic and let it fry gently for 2 minutes. Add the rest of the ingredients to the pan and stir over the heat for 2 3 minutes just so that all of the ingredients become well slicked in the oil and mixed thoroughly.

**Increase** the heat to maximum and when you hear a sizzle, tip the steaming pasta and broccoli into the pan. Toss well so that all of the pasta is coated with the oil.

**Season** with salt and pepper – you may need to go lightly on the salt because of the anchovies, but it is almost impossible to add too much freshly ground black pepper to this dish.

*Tip: If you crave a little texture in this dish, just fry up some breadcrumbs in a little olive oil until they turn golden brown and sprinkle atop your dish, along with a little grated lemon zest.*

# BACON AND PEA SPAGHETTI

This is one of those dishes that proves it is just as easy to cook something fresh as it is to 'bing' some monstrosity in the microwave. This dish can be made in the time it takes for your spaghetti to cook, and if you pick up a quick-cook variety, that may be as little as 5 minutes.

## SERVES 2

**Spaghetti** to serve 2
(see page 23)

2 tbsp **olive oil**

3 rashers of **smoked streaky bacon**, cut into finger-size strips

150g **frozen peas**

Thumb-size piece of **Parmesan cheese** (about 40g), grated

**Bring** a large saucepan of salted water to the boil. Once boiling, add the spaghetti, encouraging it to slide into the water, and cook according to the packet instructions – it should take about 8–10 minutes, unless you're using quick-cook pasta.

**While** the pasta is cooking, heat the oil in a large frying pan over a high to medium heat. Add the sliced bacon and fry for 3–4 minutes. The bacon should begin rendering its fat and turning crisp.

**When** the spaghetti is about 2 minutes from being cooked, add the peas and carefully scoop out a mugful of the starchy cooking liquid and leave to one side (this will become the base of your sauce).

**Once** cooked, drain the spaghetti and peas through a colander and tip them straight into the pan with the frying bacon. Pour in a quarter of the mug of cooking liquid along with the grated Parmesan. Reduce the heat to the lowest setting, and then mix well until you achieve a delicious and creamy pasta dish.

**Variation:** *Use this recipe as a base for other flavour combinations – add something as simple as a squeeze of lemon, finely chopped parsley or some pre-cooked chicken and this dish will take on a whole new level of taste and sophistication.*

# PAPPARDELLE CARBONARA

Forget any idea of stodgy mushroom-and-bacon pub plates of so-called carbonara – they are but a distant and disfigured evil cousin of what should be a light, satisfying and quick meal.

## SERVES 1

1 tbsp **olive oil**

2 rashers of **streaky bacon**, chopped

100g **pappardelle**

1 **egg**

Thumb-size piece of **Parmesan cheese** (about 40g), grated

Small handful of **fresh parsley**, chopped (optional)

**Salt** and **pepper**

**Variation:** *You don't strictly need to use pappardelle. Any kind of pasta you have in the cupboard will do just fine.*

**Heat** the oil in a frying pan over a medium to high heat. Once hot, add the chopped bacon and fry gently, stirring occasionally, for 4–5 minutes. The bacon should be cooked and golden. Remove the cooked bacon and place on a piece of kitchen paper to drain any excess oil. Set aside.

**Bring** a large saucepan of salted water to the boil. Add the pappardelle and cook according to the packet instructions – it should take about 8–10 minutes.

**While** the pasta is boiling, crack the egg into a bowl and add the grated Parmesan. Season with a little salt and a generous amount of freshly ground black pepper and whisk with a fork so that it is all reasonably well combined.

**Just** before you drain the cooked pasta, carefully scoop out a mugful of the starchy cooking water and leave to one side.

**Drain** the pasta through a colander and immediately return it to the pan it was cooked in. Pour over your egg and Parmesan mixture and quickly stir to coat the pasta. Add a splash of the cooking water from the mug, the cooked bacon and the parsley (if using) and stir to combine. By now you should have created a velvety sauce as the heat from the cooked pasta and the cooking liquid melts the Parmesan and warms the egg through.

**Eat** straight from the saucepan, or tip into a bowl and relish your classic creation.

# SIMPLE POTATO SALAD

Here's a dish that sits well alongside almost any summer meal, barbecued meats or grilled fish — and most of the hard work (if you can call it that) is peeling the potatoes.

**SERVES 4**

3 large **potatoes,** peeled and roughly chopped into stamp-size chunks

2 **eggs**

2 **spring onions,** trimmed and finely sliced

2 heaped tbsp **mayonnaise**

**Salt** and **pepper**

**Bring** a large saucepan of salted water to the boil. Once boiling, add the potatoes and eggs, and cook for 10 minutes or until the potatoes are cooked all the way through. Remove the eggs with a slotted spoon before draining the potatoes through a colander.

**Run** the eggs under cold water until they are cool enough to handle. Peel the eggs and then roughly chop them up with a knife into small pieces.

**When** the potatoes are cool enough to handle, place them in a bowl and scrape in the chopped egg. Add the spring onions and the mayonnaise along with a generous amount of salt and pepper. Gently mix the salad together, being careful not to break up the potatoes too much.

**This** salad is the perfect accompaniment to almost any simply cooked meat and fish.

# MY FIRST CHICKEN FRICASSEE

Even if you have no interest in cooking whatsoever, and see food simply as the fuel that you must consume to stay alive between lectures and nights in the union, then this is the recipe for you.

**SERVES 2**

2 tbsp **oil**

4 **chicken thighs**, skinless and boneless, chopped into quarters

1 x 400g tin of **creamy chicken soup**

1 tbsp each of finely chopped fresh **flat-leaf parsley** and **chives** (optional)

**Cooked rice** to serve 2 (see page 22)

**Heat** the oil in a frying pan over a high heat. When hot, add the chicken pieces and fry for 3–4 minutes until they are nicely browned on all sides.

**Reduce** the heat a little and add the tin of chicken soup. Fill the tin halfway with water and swirl before pouring into the pan. Bring your fricassee up to the boil before reducing to a simmer and cooking for 5 minutes until the chicken is fully cooked.

**Triumphantly** top some steaming rice with the fricassee before opting out of adding any parsley or chives.

# CHEESY EASY OMELETTE

The omelette is beautiful simplicity. Quick, easy, cheap and versatile – all in all a student godsend. Once you get into the swing of omelette making, there's absolutely no reason why it shouldn't become a once-a-week favourite. This recipe is for a ham and cheese omelette that everybody should know how to cook.

### SERVES 2

3 **eggs**

1 tbsp **oil**

1 slice of **ham**, cut into thin strips

Thumb-sized piece of **Cheddar cheese** (about 40g), grated

**Salt** and **pepper**

- **Crack** the eggs into a bowl and season with a little salt and pepper. Heat the oil in a small non-stick frying pan over a medium to high heat. When hot, pour the beaten egg in.

- **Using** a wooden spoon or spatula, work the egg from around the sides, almost 'scrambling' it. Fry like this while stirring for about 30 seconds. Your egg by this point should be almost setting. Spread the egg out on the base of the frying pan and scatter over the sliced ham and the grated cheese.

- **Leave** the omelette frying in the pan for about 1 minute, just so the cheese begins to melt, then remove the pan from the heat. Using your wooden spoon or spatula, carefully lift up the edge closest to you and fold it over to create a semi-circle. Don't worry if it tears. Leave the omelette in the pan like this for a further 20 seconds just to let the cheese fully melt.

- **Tip** your omelette out onto a plate and enjoy.

- **Variation:** *We all know classic omelette variations such as mushrooms and tomatoes, but we suggest being a bit bolder with your ingredients. Try adding 1 teaspoon of sesame oil and 2 teaspoons of light soy sauce to the beaten egg, and instead of using ham and cheese add prawns and beansprouts to make a delicious faux foo yung.*

# EGGS PIPÉRADE

A simple dish with a funny name – it's French, so pronounce it 'peeper-ard' (roughly). This dish involves a fair amount of chopping and frying, which can seem a bit intimidating. But what you will find is that there is a natural rhythm to the recipe: the cooking time of each ingredient allows you just enough time to prep the next, so it sort of pulls you along to a delicious-tasting finale. You'll be cooking this for breakfast, lunch and dinner by the time you've finished university.

## SERVES 2

4 tbsp **oil**

1 **red onion**, peeled and finely sliced

2 **peppers**, either red or yellow (but not green), deseeded and thinly sliced

2 **garlic** cloves, peeled and finely chopped

1 fresh **thyme** sprig

1 x 400g tin of **chopped tomatoes**

1 tsp **sugar**

4 **eggs**

Handful of grated **Cheddar cheese**

Hot **buttered toast**, to serve

**Salt** and **pepper**

**Heat** the oil in a large frying pan over a medium to high heat. Once hot, add the red onion and fry for 4 minutes, stirring occasionally. Add the peppers and continue to stir and fry for a further 4 minutes. By now the onion should be taking on a little colour and softening.

**Add** the garlic and the thyme and continue frying for a further 3 minutes. At this point all the vegetables should be softened and there should be a very satisfying savoury smell coming from your pan.

**Pour** in the chopped tomatoes, then add the sugar and some salt and pepper and stir to combine. Bring the mixture up to the boil, then reduce to a light simmer. Using a wooden spoon, try to fashion 4 small gaps in the mixture in which to crack your eggs.

**Carefully** crack your eggs into the gaps you have created, trying not to break the yolks. Once all the eggs are in, sprinkle the grated Cheddar over the dish and cover the pan. If your pan doesn't come with a lid, then look for something like a large plate or a tray. It doesn't have to fit perfectly, just enough to help a little steam build up and cook the eggs.

**Simmer**, covered, for 4 minutes, before carefully lifting off the lid. Lightly poke the yolks with a spoon – they should still be soft, but the white on top should be cooked.

**Carefully** remove the eggs and the vegetable mixture onto hot buttered toast. Alternatively, dunk toasted soldiers directly into the pan and scoop.

# CHEESE AND HAM TOASTIE

Melted cheese is God's gift to the human race. There is nothing more comforting than slabs of Cheddar cheese melted on toasted bread. This recipe works just as well on a Sunday evening as it does after a big night out or, well, anytime really.

**SERVES 1**

2 tbsp **butter**, at room temperature

2 slices of **bread,** either white or brown

2 slices of **ham**

Large thumb-size piece of **Cheddar cheese** (about 60g), grated

- **Heat** a frying pan over a medium to high heat. While the pan is heating, butter both the slices of bread on one side.

- **Once** the frying pan is hot, lay one of the slices of bread, butter side down in the pan. You should begin to hear the satisfying sound of bread frying. Reduce the heat to medium.

- **Place** the slices of ham on the bread before topping with the cheese. Place the second slice of buttered bread on top, with the buttered side facing upwards.

- **Using** a spatula, press down on the sandwich a little to compress. Fry without turning for 3–4 minutes. Carefully flip the sandwich over onto its uncooked side and fry for a further 3–4 minutes, giving it an encouraging press every now and then.

- **Flip** the sandwich one last time to ensure that it is evenly and beautifully golden on both sides.

- **Serve** either on its own or alongside a squeeze of ketchup, a little (optional) salad and a huge grin.

- **Variations:** *There are endless ingredients that can go into a toastie. Add thinly sliced tomato or spinach, or substitute the ham for Multi-purpose Mince (see page 38) for savoury versions. Other tasty fillings are cheese and onion or cooked sausage and cheese. For sweet variations try hazelnut chocolate spread and banana, sliced Mars bar or peanut butter and jam.*

# SWEETCORN FRITTERS WITH AVOCADO SALSA

Some mornings when the sun is shining and you're feeling all go-getting and cosmopolitan, a fry-up seems out of place. A bowl of cereal is far too 'school morning' and toast . . . well, it's just toast really. On those days, look no further than our Antipodean-influenced sweetcorn fritters with avocado salsa to give you an imaginative start to the day.

## MAKES 6

### FOR THE SALSA

1 **avocado**, stoned, flesh scooped out and roughly broken up

2 **spring onions**, finely sliced

2 **tomatoes**, deseeded and roughly chopped

1 **lime**, juice only

**Salt** and **pepper**

### FOR THE FRITTERS

1 x 200g tin of **sweetcorn**, drained

2 **spring onions**, finely sliced

5 tbsp **self-raising flour** (about 75g)

1 **egg**

**Oil**, for frying

**Make** the salsa first, as it can stand as you prepare the fritters. Lightly mix together all of the ingredients, being careful not to turn it into a mush. Taste and season with salt and pepper.

**Prepare** the fritters. Tip the drained sweetcorn into a bowl and add the spring onions, flour, egg and a generous amount of salt and pepper. Mix together to form a smooth pouring batter, adding a little water if needed.

**Pour** enough oil into a frying pan to cover the base and heat over a medium to high heat. Once hot, begin dolloping in mounds of the batter using a couple of tablespoons. Form and size doesn't have to be perfect, but consistency will help you judge the cooking time better.

**Fry** each little fritter for 2–3 minutes until golden, before flipping carefully. Continue to cook for a further 2–3 minutes, before removing to a piece of kitchen paper to absorb any excess oil.

**Repeat** the process with the remaining batter.

**Serve** the fritters topped with the salsa, and if you listen carefully you will hear your stomach singing the dawn chorus.

# DUCK NOODLE STIR-FRY

Everybody loves crispy aromatic duck from the takeaway, but it is more often than not the most expensive dish on the menu. So when you're craving the sweet, dark flavours of Southeast Asia, try our version. It's quicker, and ultimately more satisfying because we've added noodles. Once all the ingredients are prepared, this dish should take you just over 5 minutes to cook.

## SERVES 2

2 tbsp **oil**

1 **duck breast**, fat removed and sliced into thin strips

1 tsp **five-spice powder**

2 **spring onions**, trimmed and finely sliced

¼ **cucumber**, sliced into thin 3cm batons

2 x nests of **dried egg noodles**, rehydrated according to packet instructions or ½ x 400g packet of **ready-to-use noodles**

2 tbsp **hoisin sauce**

**Soy sauce**, to serve

**Heat** the oil in a large frying pan or wok over a high heat. Once hot, add the slices of duck and fry for 2 minutes, stirring frequently. Reduce the heat to medium and add the five-spice powder. Continue cooking and stirring for a further minute.

**Return** the heat to maximum and toss in the spring onions and cucumber. Stir-fry for another minute before adding the noodles. Toss the noodles in the pan so that all ingredients are well incorporated, then pour in the hoisin sauce. Continue to toss and fry for a further minute and drizzle with soy sauce before serving.

**Either** dish up piles of steaming noodles for yourself and another lucky person or alternatively find a quiet place, eat straight from the pan and revel in your handiwork.

# HUNGRY BUT PENNILESS

The high times of getting a new loan or pay cheque wait just around the corner; you're busy imagining how you are going to blow the cash as soon as it's arrived in your account. But for now you can only window-shop at the supermarket meat counter, and the campus canteen may as well be The Ritz.

Well, fear not, as the following chapter is dedicated solely to recipes that can be bought with the coins down the back of your sofa (they're there, really take a look). Not only will they satisfy your bank manager and your grumbling tummy, but they will also more than satisfy your taste buds, as we use all our nous to eke out maximum flavour from minimum budget.

If times are particularly tough then may we also suggest you share the economic burden with one of your buddies, as many of the following recipes cater for more than one hungry mouth.

# TOMATOES ON TOAST

The Italians traditionally prepared bruschetta to showcase their olive oils. We're cooking our version because it's cheap and really, really tasty. The ingredients cost very little, so if possible try to spend a little extra on the bread. It really will make a difference.

## SERVES 2

3 large **tomatoes**

½ tsp dried **oregano**

Drizzle of **olive oil**

2 slices of good-quality **bread** (sourdough or similar)

1 **garlic** clove, peeled and left whole

**Salt** and **pepper**

**Preheat** the oven to 200°C (gas mark 6).

**Slice** your tomatoes in half and place them on a baking tray. Season the tomatoes with salt and pepper, sprinkle evenly with the dried oregano and drizzle with a little olive oil. Bake the tomatoes in the oven for 15 minutes. They should still be holding their shape, but be tender.

**Meanwhile**, toast your bread. Once toasted, rub each slice with the whole garlic – the rough edge of the toasted bread will act as a grater and the bread will be deliciously infused with garlic. Drizzle the toast with a little olive oil and place on a plate.

**Top** the toast with the baked tomatoes. Sit back and enjoy one of the simplest and most delicious dishes on the planet.

# PROPER CHEESE ON TOAST

This has to be one of the most popular comfort dishes. Forget about limp bread with melted Cheddar cheese on top; this is the way cheese on toast should be done, and as such it should be treated with respect and only served to your nearest and dearest.

## SERVES 2

Knob of **butter**

2 tbsp **plain flour**

200ml **milk**

200g **Cheddar cheese**, grated

1 tsp **mustard** (English, Dijon or wholegrain)

1 **egg yolk**

4 thick slices of **toasted farmhouse bread**

**Salad** and **Worcestershire sauce**, to serve (optional)

**Tip:** *Once all the cheese, mustard and egg has been added to the sauce, you can leave it to cool completely and place in the fridge for the next day. When you come to use it, it will be almost solid. Just break up pieces and place on top of the toasted bread before grilling for a little longer.*

**Preheat** your grill to its maximum setting.

**Melt** the butter in a saucepan over a medium to high heat. Once fully melted, add the flour and stir well with a wooden spoon to incorporate. Cook like this, stirring regularly, for 1 minute.

**Take** the pan off the heat and pour in a quarter of the milk. Stir well with a wooden spoon until the flour mix has absorbed the milk. Pour in another quarter of the milk and stir again before placing the saucepan back on the heat and adding the remaining milk. Stir the mixture thoroughly while bringing it up to the boil.

**Once** the sauce is boiling, reduce the heat to minimum and add the cheese a little at a time, stirring constantly, to ensure the cheese melts into the sauce. Once all of the cheese has been incorporated, take the saucepan off the heat and beat in both the mustard and the egg yolk.

**Let** the mixture cool a little (see Tip) before spooning generous amounts onto your toasted bread. Place the topped slices under the grill and cook for about 5 minutes until the cheese mixture is bubbling and golden. Keep an eye on it to ensure it doesn't burn.

**Serve** your Proper Cheese on Toast along with a little salad and lashings of Worcestershire sauce (if using) to yourself and a friend and enjoy the silence that will fall as you both tuck into the scrumptious snack.

# POSH BEANS ON TOAST

There is nothing that we at studentbeans.com aren't afraid to pimp or mess with, even our humble namesake.

## SERVES 2

1 x 420g tin of **baked beans**

1 tsp **sugar**

4 tsp **Worcestershire sauce**

Few drops of **Tabasco sauce**

½ tsp **Marmite**

**Butter**, for spreading

2 slices of good-quality **toasted bread**

**Pour** your beans into a saucepan and heat them, as you have done a million times before, over a medium heat. Add all of the remaining ingredients and stir well to combine.

**Bring** the beans up to the boil, stirring regularly, before serving on slices of generously buttered toast.

# GARLIC MUSHROOMS ON TOAST

This is one of those forgotten classics that is too good to be lost in the ether. So tasty, so satisfying and so easy.

## SERVES 2

1 tbsp **butter**

1 tsp **oil**

½ x 350g pack of **mushrooms**, halved

1 **garlic** clove, peeled and finely chopped

2 tbsp freshly chopped **parsley** (optional)

2 slices of **toasted bread**

**Salt** and **pepper**

**Heat** the butter and oil in a frying pan over a medium to high heat. Once melted and bubbling, add the mushrooms and fry for 2–3 minutes, stirring regularly.

**Reduce** the heat a little before adding the garlic. Continue to fry, stirring, for 2 minutes. The mushrooms should start to take on a little colour in this time.

**Season** the mushrooms generously with salt and pepper, before adding the chopped parsley (if using). Stir one last time before piling the tasty mushrooms onto freshly toasted bread.

# CARB-LOADED PESTO PASTA

Once you've read this recipe, you're going to think that we've either lost our tiny minds or have included a 'joke' recipe. As soon as you've cooked it, you will think we are geniuses. The combination of potatoes and pasta has been enjoyed in Italy for decades under the name Genovese. The cooked potatoes transform into a silky smooth sauce for the pasta, flavoured by the pesto. We don't think we need to tell you that this is a tummy-filler.

**SERVES 2**

1 large **potato**, peeled and roughly chopped into 2cm chunks

**Spaghetti** to serve 2 (see page 23)

1 x 200g pack of **green beans**, trimmed and halved

½ jar of **green pesto** (about 95g)

Thumb-size piece of **Parmesan cheese** (about 50g), grated

**Salt** and **pepper**

**Bring** a large saucepan of salted water to boiling point, add the potato and boil for about 5 minutes before adding the spaghetti. Boil the spaghetti according to the packet instructions – it should take about 8–10 minutes. When your pasta has 2 minutes of cooking time to go, add the halved green beans.

**Just** before you drain the ingredients, carefully scoop out a mugful of the starchy cooking water and leave to one side. Drain the potatoes, pasta and beans through a colander and tip back into the pan off the heat.

**In** a bowl, mix the saved cooking liquid, the green pesto and the Parmesan together. Tip this mixture into the pan with the other ingredients and mix well, allowing the potatoes to break up a little.

**Season** well with salt and pepper before piling steaming mounds of delicious carbs onto warm plates.

# TUNA PASTA BAKE

In the student dinner hall of fame, this dish stands proud. Thank you, tuna pasta bake, for combining essential carbs and protein in one cheap and tasty package, and for powering students across the land through their masses of work and even more play.

**SERVES 4**

325g **pasta** (we like rigatoni or penne)

1 head of **broccoli florets** separated, stalks roughly chopped

1 quantity **White Sauce** (see pages 30–31)

Large thumb-size piece of **Cheddar cheese** (about 75g), grated

Thumb-size piece of **Parmesan cheese** (about 50g), grated

1 x 200g tin of **tuna**, drained

**Preheat** the oven to 190°C (gas mark 5).

**Bring** a large saucepan of salted water to boiling point, add the pasta and cook according to the packet instructions – it should take about 8–10 minutes. When the pasta is about 5 minutes from being cooked, add the broccoli stalks. Cook for 3 minutes, then add the broccoli florets. Cook for a further 2 minutes before draining all the pasta and broccoli through a colander and leaving under cold running water to cool.

**Make** the White Sauce according to the method on pages 30–31. Once the sauce has thickened, add half of the grated Cheddar and Parmesan. Stir well until melted and fully combined.

**Pour** enough cheese sauce into the bottom of a 28cm x 15cm ovenproof dish to lightly cover the base. Tumble in half of the cooled pasta and broccoli before flaking the tuna over the top. Pour over a couple more spoonfuls of the cheese sauce before piling the remaining pasta and broccoli on top. Now evenly pour over the remaining cheese sauce. It doesn't overly matter if some of the pasta is not covered with sauce – these will become the crispy bits later.

**Sprinkle** over the remaining cheese and bake in the oven for 30 minutes until the top is golden brown and the sauce is bubbling.

**Serve** with a huge smile on your face.

# SAUSAGE AND TOMATO SPAGHETTI

Carbs, protein and veg wrapped up in a familiar and homely-tasting recipe – the perfect culinary package. This one has the potential to become a weekly 'best friend' staple.

## SERVES 4

6 pork **sausages**

24 cherry **tomatoes**

**Spaghetti** to serve 4 (see page 23)

2 tbsp **olive oil**

**Salt** and **pepper**

**Heat** the grill to just below maximum. Place the sausages on the grill tray and cook for about 12 minutes, turning a couple of times, until they are totally cooked through.

**About** 5 minutes from the end of cooking the sausages, carefully place the cherry tomatoes on the same tray and place under the grill.

**While** the sausages are cooking, bring a large saucepan of salted water to the boil. Once boiling, add the spaghetti and gently encourage it all into the water as it becomes softened by the heat. Cook the spaghetti according to the packet instructions – this should take about 8–10 minutes.

**Once** cooked, drain the spaghetti through a colander, then tip back into the pan. Add the oil and some seasoning, before mixing well and leaving to one side as you tend to your sausages.

**By** now your sausages should be fully cooked through and the tomatoes just a little shrivelled and coloured. Tumble the tomatoes in with the waiting spaghetti. Carefully transfer the sausages to a plate/chopping board/clean bit of work surface and roughly slice into 1cm pieces. Add these pieces to the pasta and tomatoes.

**Mix** all the ingredients together thoroughly, squishing the tomatoes as you go, creating a deliciously sweet sauce for the spaghetti. Test the seasoning and serve.

**Variation:** *If your budget doesn't stretch as far as sweet cherry tomatoes, then simply substitute with two normal-sized tomatoes, sliced into quarters and seasoned with salt and pepper a little before grilling. You might have to grill them for a couple of minutes extra to help break down the flesh to the point when they can be easily crushed with the back of a fork.*

# BEAN CASSOULET

Cassoulet is so traditionally French that you can almost imagaine it wearing a beret. The classic version involves a whole pile of meat and some mystic chanting. You'll be happy to know that here the meat has been omitted to make this hearty dish both affordable and vegetarian. You can make up your own mind on the chanting.

## SERVES 4

3 tbsp **oil**

1 **onion**, peeled and diced

2 **celery** sticks, diced

1 large **carrot**, peeled and diced

2 **garlic** cloves, peeled and finely chopped

3 fresh **thyme** sprigs

2 dried **bay leaves**

1 tbsp **balsamic vinegar**

½ glass of **red wine**

2 x 400g tins of **chopped tomatoes**

200ml **vegetable stock**

1 x 400g tin of **cannellini beans**, rinsed and drained

2 x 400g tins of **butter beans**

Small handful of grated **Parmesan cheese** (about 70g)

Small handful of **breadcrumbs** (optional)

**Salt** and **pepper**

**Preheat** the oven to 200°C (gas mark 6).

**Heat** the oil in a large saucepan over a medium to high heat. Once hot, add the onion, celery and carrot. Fry the mixture, stirring regularly, for 8 minutes until the vegetables have softened. Add the chopped garlic, thyme and bay leaves and continue to fry for a further 3 minutes before pouring in the vinegar and red wine and letting it reduce to almost nothing.

**Pour** the tinned tomatoes into the saucepan. Fill one of the empty tins with vegetable stock and tip that in too. Bring the mixture to the boil before tipping in the beans. Let the mixture come back to the boil before reducing to a simmer and cooking like this for 5 minutes. Season generously with salt and pepper.

**Pour** the mixture into an ovenproof dish and scatter with the grated Parmesan and breadcrumbs (if using). Bake in the preheated oven for 20 minutes, until the Parmesan is golden and bubbling.

**Serve** on its own or with a light salad amidst Gallic chanting.

# CURRIED POTATOES

When times are tough and the next student loan cheque seems light years away, you want a dish that's going to cost almost nothing, fill you up and satisfy the taste buds. Look no further than our curried potatoes.

## SERVES 2

2 floury **potatoes** (such as Maris Piper or King Edward), peeled and roughly chopped

3 tbsp **oil**

1 tsp **cumin seeds**

2 **garlic** cloves, peeled and finely chopped

1 **red chilli**, deseeded and finely chopped

1 tbsp **garam masala**

2 **spring onions**, trimmed and finely sliced

Handful of **spinach** (about 200g)

**Salt** and **pepper**

### TO SERVE

2 **fried eggs**

2 tbsp freshly chopped **coriander**

**Bring** a large saucepan of salted water to the boil. Once boiling, add the chopped potatoes and boil for about 8 minutes until cooked all the way through. This can be tested by pushing a fork into a chunk of potato; when it's ready the fork should pierce the potato easily. Once cooked, drain the potatoes through a colander and waft them around a little to dry them off.

**Heat** the oil in a frying pan over a high heat. Once hot, add the cooked potatoes and leave them to sizzle, turning a couple of times for 6–7 minutes until they are browning all over. Reduce the heat to medium before adding the cumin seeds, garlic and chopped red chilli. Fry the mixture, turning occasionally, for 3 minutes (you want the potatoes to be crispy on the outside).

**Sprinkle** over the garam masala, toss to coat the potatoes evenly and fry for a further 2 minutes. Add a little extra oil if the potatoes begin to stick.

**Add** the spring onions and fry for another minute before heaping in the spinach and seasoning to taste. Gently turn the potatoes and spinach until the spinach has completely wilted.

**Serve** the steaming curried potatoes topped with a fried egg per person and sprinkled with coriander.

# BACON AND LENTIL SOUP

Lentils have long been known as hippy food. Well, although it's turned out that achieving world peace is going to take a bit more than sitting in a tepee naked, those crazy hippies were onto something with lentils – cheap, filling and also darn good for you ... In fact, if everybody managed to get lentils into their weekly diet, it would probably be a helpful first step towards global peace, love and understanding. Right on.

## SERVES 4

**Oil**, for frying

1 **onion**, peeled and finely diced

2 **carrots**, peeled and finely diced

2 **celery** sticks, peeled and finely diced

200g **smoked pancetta** cubes or **smoked streaky bacon** sliced into thin strips

250g **puy lentils** (the green ones)

1.5 litres **chicken** or **vegetable stock**

4 tbsp freshly chopped **parsley** (optional)

**Salt** and **pepper**

**Heat** the oil in a large saucepan over a high heat. Once hot, add the onion and fry for 3–5 minutes until lightly softened. Add the carrots, celery and pancetta. Keep frying for a further 6 minutes, stirring regularly. If the vegetables look like they are starting to burn, just turn the heat down a little.

**Once** all of the vegetables have softened and the pancetta has cooked through a little, add the lentils and stock. Stir all the ingredients a couple of times. Bring the soup to the boil and then reduce the heat and simmer for 20–30 minutes until the lentils are tender. Taste the soup and adjust the seasoning if needed.

**Stir** through the parsley (if using) just before serving the steaming and satisfying soup in large bowls with a big helping of peace and love, man.

# OLD-SCHOOL SAUSAGES AND LENTILS

More bloody lentils? Well, guess what! Here's another lentil recipe, and this one is better than the last, because it includes sausages. It is worth buying flavoured sausages for this recipe. You can still buy them from the supermarket, but maybe go a notch up in quality from the normal pink specimens, just this once.

**SERVES 4**

3 tbsp **olive oil**

6 **sausages**

1 **red onion**, peeled and finely diced

2 **celery** sticks, finely diced

2 **garlic** cloves, peeled and finely chopped

1 **fresh thyme** sprig

3 **tomatoes**, roughly chopped into quarters

300g **puy lentils**

750ml–1 litre **chicken** or **vegetable stock**

**Heat** half the olive oil in a frying pan over a high heat. Once hot, add the sausages and brown all over. Once they are browned, remove the sausages to a plate and leave to cool.

**Heat** the remaining oil in a large saucepan over a medium to high heat. Once hot, add the red onion and fry, stirring occasionally, for 3 minutes. Add the celery and garlic and continue to fry, stirring occasionally, for a further 3 minutes before adding the thyme. By now the onions and celery should have softened.

**Tumble** in the chopped tomatoes along with the lentils and the browned sausages. Stir to mix before pouring in the stock. Bring the liquid to the boil before reducing the heat to a simmer, covering with a lid and cooking for 15 minutes. Remove the lid and continue cooking for 20–30 minutes. By now the liquid should have reduced a little and the lentils should be cooked and tender.

**Spoon** steaming mounds into bowls and watch as your friends are converted to lentils in front of your very eyes.

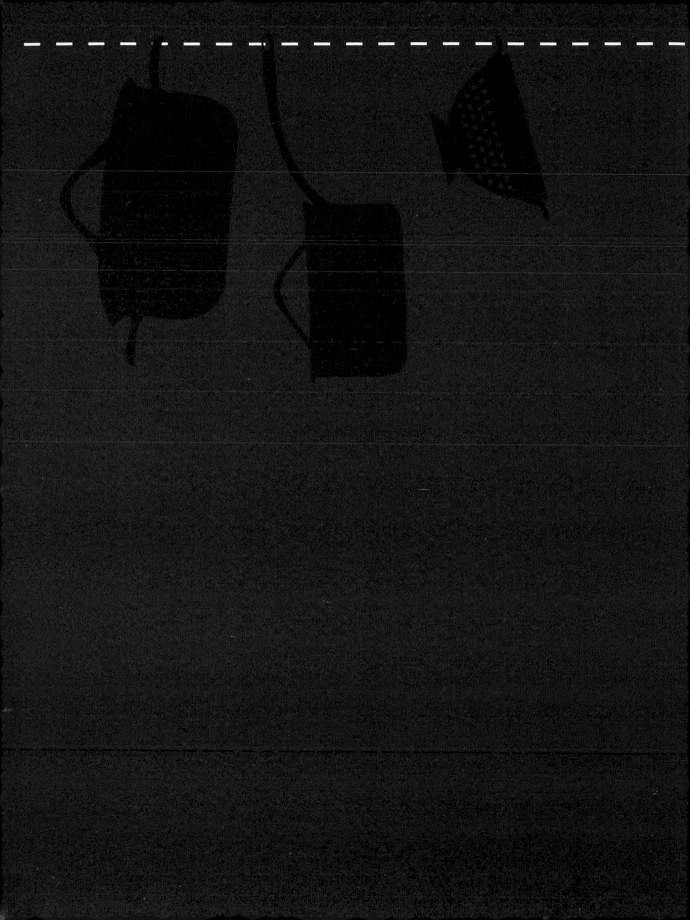

# HOME-COOKED CLASSICS

Nobody cooks like your mum. Her culinary position in your life has been cemented over many years of delicious dishes that have mended broken hearts, cured colds and celebrated birthdays.

We would never suggest that we could take your mum's place, and those dishes that mean so much to you may be best learned from her. But what we have done is to compile a chapter's worth of warmth and taste that may go some way to transporting you back to those sacred meals you enjoyed at home.

For those of you whose mum's were really bad at cooking, when you're missing a bit of TLC, look no further than this chapter. Let the food envelope you in a cuddly and delicious embrace, then overflow with nostalgia for the home cooking you never had.

# CHICKEN DINNER IN A TRAY

Straightforward to cook, simple to clean up, deliciously warming and reasonably healthy . . . you couldn't ask for anything more.

## SERVES 4

4 tbsp **olive oil**

2 **potatoes**, washed, sliced in half lengthways and into wedges

6 **chicken thighs**, skin on and bone in

3 fresh **thyme sprigs**, leaves only

1 **red onion**, peeled and roughly chopped into wedges

4 **garlic** cloves, left whole but bashed with your palm

12 **cherry tomatoes** or 3 normal tomatoes, quartered

Large handful of **baby spinach** (about 100g), washed (optional)

**Salt** and **pepper**

**Preheat** the oven to 200°C (gas mark 6).

**Drizzle** a roasting tray with the oil. Scatter the potato wedges on the tray, season with salt and pepper and mix around with your hands so all the potato is coated in the oil. Roast in the preheated oven for 20 minutes.

**Remove** the tray from the oven and add the chicken thighs, skin-side down. Return to the oven and cook for a further 15 minutes.

Take the tray out of the oven and scatter over the thyme, red onion and garlic cloves. Mix around a little with a spoon and turn the chicken skin-side up, before returning to the oven for a further 15 minutes.

**Finally**, remove the tray from the oven again and dot the tomatoes around the potatoes and chicken. Put your tray back in the oven and roast for a further 8 minutes.

**Divide** the spinach between serving plates and top with a little of everything from the roasting tray.

**Serve** up to appreciative friends. If they don't show appreciation, they are not real friends and should be replaced as soon as possible.

# EASY CHICKEN STEW

Chicken breasts are the worst part of a chicken – gastronomically and economically they make absolutely no sense. They shrivel up to a dry matter that is scientifically closer to cardboard than meat, and they charge you for the displeasure. Stick to thighs and legs that are best bought with the bone in and skin on. However, you may find yourself too squeamish for this, in which case start with the boneless and skinless variety and go on from there – I promise you will be converted as soon as you realise how much money you will save.

## SERVES 2

3 tbsp **oil**

4 **chicken thighs**, skin on and bone in

1 **red onion**, peeled and roughly chopped as small as your patience can stand

2 rashers of **smoked bacon**, chopped

2 **fresh thyme** sprigs

1 dried **bay leaf**

3 **tomatoes**, quartered

1 litre **chicken stock**

2 large **potatoes**, peeled and chopped into large chunks

small bunch of **flat-leaf parsley**, chopped, to garnish

**Salt** and **pepper**

£££
per person

**Heat** half the oil in a large saucepan (or a fancy casserole dish) over a medium to high heat. Once hot, add your chicken thighs, skin-side down. They should sizzle lightly as you place them in the hot oil. It is important that the chicken pieces are only one layer deep. If your pan is not big enough then you may have to either halve the recipe or brown the meat in batches.

**While** the thighs are browning, season the flesh side of the chicken with salt and pepper. There will be an urge to turn the thighs constantly – do not. Leave the meat to brown on each side for about 4 minutes without prodding or moving. Turning the meat simply reduces the heat in the pan and on the flesh, which will result in insipid meat and very little flavour. It may take a little more or less time than stated, but you are aiming for a lovely dark, caramel-brown colour to the meat. Once this is achieved, remove the thighs to a clean plate and leave to rest while you continue with the vegetables. Drain off any excess fat that has rendered from the chicken.

**Reduce** the heat to medium and pour the remaining oil into the pan the chicken was browned in. Add the onion and cook, stirring frequently, for 4 minutes until just softened. Increase the heat a little and add the bacon pieces. Continue to fry and stir for a further 3–4 minutes – by this point the bacon and onion should be just beginning to take on a little colour. Add the thyme, bay leaf and tomato quarters and fry for a further minute. Your work should be paying off by now, as there should be a delicious smell emanating from your pan.

**Slide** the chicken thighs back into the pan, along with any juices that have leaked onto the plate. Pour in the stock and give everything a good stir to mix everything together. Bring the casserole to the boil, then reduce the heat to a simmer – the liquid should appear to be burping every now and then, and no more. Cook, uncovered, for about 25 minutes.

**Add** the peeled and chopped potato – it may be necessary to increase the heat a little to bring the stew back to a simmer. Continue to cook until the potato is tender – about a further 12 minutes.

**Check** the seasoning before serving in large bowls and garnishing with chopped parsley.

# CHICKEN PILAF

Food can be such an effective portal to past memories; be it a roast taking you back to Sundays with the family or fizzy cola bottles reminding you of your childhood. This dish is so powerful it's going to take you all the way back to a place that you can't remember, but you know was safe – the womb. With every mouthful, you'll feel a warm and fuzzy calm sweeping over you.

## SERVES 4

3 tbsp **oil**

6 **chicken thighs**, skin on and bone in

2 rashers of **smoked streaky bacon**, sliced

1 **leek,** washed, trimmed and sliced into 1cm rounds

250g **basmati rice**

650ml **chicken** or **vegetable stock**

Knob of **butter** (optional)

1 tbsp each of freshly chopped **parsley** and **chives** (optional)

**Salt** and **pepper**

**Preheat** the oven to 180°C (gas mark 4).

**Heat** 2 tablespoons of the oil in a large casserole dish over a medium to high heat. Season the chicken all over with salt and pepper. Once the oil is hot, add the thighs skin side down and cook for 4 minutes until brown. Turn the chicken over and fry for a further 4 minutes. Remove the browned chicken to a clean plate to rest while you continue with the recipe.

**Pour** the remaining oil into the pan the chicken was cooked in and return to the heat. Add the bacon and leek and fry, stirring regularly, for 4 minutes. The bacon should be cooked through and the leek beginning to soften. Tip the chicken thighs back into the pan along with any of the juices that may have collected on the plate.

**Tip** in the rice and stir to mix. Pour in the stock and stir again so that all the ingredients are well combined. Bring the liquid up to the boil before clamping on a lid and placing in the preheated oven for 25 minutes.

**Remove** the casserole from the oven and take off the lid. Stir in the butter and the herbs (if using).

**Pile** the chicken and rice high on plates and share with friends. Feel yourself slowly curling up into the foetal position with every mouthful you take.

**Tip:** *If you don't have an ovenproof dish, then simply simmer it on the hob with a tight-fitting lid. Just cook over a very low heat. Add a little more water to ensure the rice doesn't 'cook dry' and burn on the bottom and let the rice cook for a further 10 minutes.*

# HEARTY FISH PIE

Fish pie is all about luxurious comfort. The indulgent ingredients are bound together with a more humble sauce – the combination of rich and poor takes us all to a very happy place.

## SERVES 4

1 litre **milk**

2 dried **bay leaves**

1 **onion**, peeled and roughly chopped

250g **smoked haddock**

250g **skinless haddock**

1 portion of **Mashed Potato** (see page 19)

2 **egg yolks**

40g **butter**

1 **leek**, washed, trimmed and chopped into thin rounds

40g **plain flour**

80g **Parmesan** cheese, grated

3 tbsp freshly chopped **parsley**

8 large, raw **king prawns**

**Boiled peas**, to serve

**Salt** and **pepper**

**Preheat** the oven to 200°C (gas mark 6).

**Pour** the milk into a saucepan and add the bay leaves and onion. Add 500ml water and bring to the boil. Reduce the heat and leave to simmer for 2 minutes. Place both the haddocks into the liquid and leave to simmer for 1 minute before turning off the heat and leaving to cool.

**Make** your mashed potato following the instructions on page 19. While the mashed potato is still warm, beat in the 2 egg yolks. Beat quickly to avoid scrambled egg in your mash.

**Once** the fish and liquid has cooled enough to handle, strain the mixture through a colander into a bowl (not down the sink!). Do not discard the liquid, just the bits of onion and the bay leaves. Flake the fish with your fingers into the base of an ovenproof dish (or 4 small separate dishes), discarding any skin.

**Measure** out 600ml of the flavoured milk and discard the rest.

**Melt** the butter in a saucepan over a medium to high heat. Once melted and bubbling, add the chopped leek and cook, stirring regularly for 4–5 minutes until just softened. Scatter in the flour and mix well to combine. Cook the flour and butter over this heat for 1 minute.

**Remove** the pan from the heat, pour in a quarter of your flavoured milk and stir to combine. Add another quarter only when the initial milk has been absorbed by the flour, and stir again to combine. Place the pan back over a medium heat and pour in the remaining milk, stirring constantly with a wooden spoon to avoid a lumpy sauce. Bring the sauce up to the boil before adding the grated Parmesan, a little salt and a generous amount of black pepper. Once everything is well combined, remove the pan from the heat and stir in the chopped parsley.

- **Scatter** the prawns evenly over the flaked fish. Pour over your delicious white sauce. Leave to cool for 10 minutes before topping with the mashed potato.

- **Bake** in the preheated oven for 20 minutes until the top is golden and the sides are bubbling.

- **Serve** your fish pie along with some boiled peas.

# MOMMA'S MEATBALLS AND SPAGHETTI

*'Just like Momma used to make, but a thousand times better, because Momma used to open a tin and pour the meatballs onto toast.'  Mike, Southampton University*

We may have made that quote up. But we are sure there are many Mike's out there whose experience of meatballs came from the tin via the microwave. If so, welcome to an entirely new world, where 'meatballs' isn't a dirty word, it's a glorious one.

## SERVES 4

500g **minced beef**

½ an **onion**, peeled and finely diced

6 tbsp fresh **breadcrumbs**

1 **egg**, beaten

**Spaghetti** to serve 4 (see page 23)

2 tbsp **olive oil**

**Salt** and **pepper**

## FOR THE SAUCE

2 tbsp **olive oil**

1 **red onion**, peeled and finely diced

2 **garlic** cloves, peeled and finely chopped

1 fresh **thyme** sprig

1 x 400g tin of **chopped tomatoes**

Small bunch of fresh **basil**, finely chopped

1 tbsp **caster sugar**

**Start** by making the sauce. Heat the oil in a large saucepan over a medium to high heat. Once hot, add the red onion and cook for about 8–10 minutes, stirring regularly. If the onions begin to stick and colour then reduce the heat a little.

**Once** the onions are nicely softened, add the garlic and thyme and continue to cook for a further 3 minutes, stirring occasionally, before tipping in the chopped tomatoes. Half fill the emptied tomato tin with water and swirl around the sides to collect all the tomato that has been left in the tin, then pour it into the saucepan.

**Add** half of the chopped basil, the sugar and a generous amount of salt and pepper. Bring the sauce up to the boil, then reduce to a simmer. The sauce can be left to reduce while you prepare the meatballs.

**Put** the mince, onion, breadcrumbs and some salt and pepper in a bowl and mix with your hands to combine. Pour in half of the beaten egg and mix again. At this point remove a golf-ball-size lump of mixture from the bowl and try to shape it into a meatball. If it doesn't hold together easily, the mixture will need some more egg. Add the remaining egg if needed and mix to combine. You should now have a meatball mixture that is moist, but holds its shape.

**Roll** out as many golf-ball-size meatballs as possible from your mixture, placing them on a baking tray or a plate as you go. They don't have to be perfect, as all bits of meat will end up in the mixture anyway!

**Once** you have finished, carefully place the meatballs into the simmering cooking sauce. It may look like you have too many balls for the pan, but it is amazing how many can fit into a small amount of sauce. If it definitely doesn't look like there is enough sauce, then just add some water, but be sure to bring the sauce back up to a simmer before adding the meatballs. Use a spoon to lightly jimmy the balls about. Once all the meatballs are in, increase the heat and bring the sauce back up to the boil. Then reduce to a simmer again for 15 minutes.

**This** leaves just enough time to cook your spaghetti. Bring a large saucepan of salted water to boiling point and add your spaghetti, helping it to soften into the steamy water. Cook according to the packet instructions – this should take about 8–10 minutes – then drain through a colander. Tip the spaghetti back into the pan it was cooked in and mix in the oil and season lightly with salt and pepper.

**Just** before serving, add the remaining chopped basil to the meatball sauce and mix through. Proudly serve lashings of meatballs over your cooked spaghetti straight to Momma.

# CUP-A-SOUP MUSHROOM RISOTTO

Where chefs rely on combinations of butter, cheese and cream to enrich their risottos, we suggest you use a sachet of ever-lasting creamy mushroom Cup a Soup. Because of the rehydrating property of the stock, this recipe is a great way to use up some of the shrivelled mushrooms lurking at the back of the fridge. In fact, as mushrooms dehydrate they intensify in flavour, making a more delicious risotto.

**SERVES 4**

4 tbsp **olive oil**

½ an **onion**, peeled and finely diced

1 x 250g pack of **field mushrooms**, cleaned and roughly chopped

250g **risotto rice**

½ glass of **white wine** (optional)

750–900ml **vegetable** or **chicken stock**

2 x sachets of **cream of mushroom Cup a Soup**

**Heat** half the oil in a saucepan over a medium heat. Once hot, add the diced onions and cook for about 5 minutes until they have softened and are slightly coloured.

**Increase** the heat and add the rest of the oil along with the mushrooms. Fry for 2–3 minutes, stirring. Pour the rice in and continue to fry for a further minute. Stir the rice so that it is all coated in the oil and mixed well with the mushrooms and onion. Pour in the wine at this point (if using) and let it simmer down until almost totally evaporated.

**Reduce** the heat a little before pouring in a ladle or two of the stock. Wait until it has come to the boil, then, using a wooden spoon, begin to stir continuously at a steady pace (you will be doing quite a lot of stirring). Continue stirring until almost all of the stock has been absorbed before pouring in another ladle or two. Repeat the process until all of the stock has been used up, your arm is a little sore and you have a loose-looking risotto made up of tender rice and mushrooms ready for their final flourish.

**Turn** the heat down to minimum and, while still stirring, pour in the contents of both Cup a Soup sachets. Stir in the powder until it has produced a lovely creamy consistency. At this point you may want to add a little bit of water to loosen the risotto. Serve immediately.

**Any** leftover risotto can be refrigerated for up to 3 days. To reheat, add to the saucepan with a little water and bring to the boil. Simmer for 2–3 minutes to ensure all the rice is heated through.

**Variation:** *This dish can be served up as a hangover-curing plate of carbs, or you can throw in some finely chopped green herbs (such as tarragon, parsley or chives) at the end and serve with a roast chicken breast to transform it into a dish worthy of candlelight.*

- **Tip:** *If you have leftover risotto, try the following: cling film*
- *the base of a high-sided dish and pour the remaining risotto*
- *into it. Pat it down to create a flat surface. Once the risotto has*
- *completely cooled, cling film the top and place in the fridge to*
- *cool overnight. The next day, remove the top layer of cling film*
- *and flip the dish onto a chopping board. It should all come out*
- *as one large 'cake'. Remove the rest of the cling film and chop*
- *the risotto into large squares. Fry in an oiled pan over a high*
- *heat for about 2 minutes on each side. Serve with a green salad*
- *for a very satisfying lunch.*

# MAC 'N' CHEESE

How could we have even conceived of writing a student cookbook without the cheap and cheerful macaroni cheese? When funds are low and you're missing the luxuries of home, cook this up and get an instant cure.

**SERVES 3**

500g **macaroni**

1 quantity of **cheese sauce** (see pages 30–31)

Generous splash of **milk**

Handful of grated **Cheddar and Parmesan cheese**, for sprinkling

2 **tomatoes**, thinly sliced

**Salt** and **pepper**

**Preheat** the oven to 200°C (gas mark 6).

**Bring** a large saucepan of lightly salted water to boiling point. Tip in the macaroni and cook according to the packet instructions or for about 8–10 minutes until al dente.

**Once** cooked, drain through a colander, then tip straight into a ovenproof dish. Pour the prepared cheese sauce over the pasta, add a good splash of milk and turn with a spoon so that the pasta is well coated in sauce.

**Sprinkle** over the cheese, then top with slices of tomato and season. Bake in the preheated oven for 15–20 minutes until golden and bubbling.

**Variation:** *Cooked streaky bacon, fried mushrooms, sweetcorn, truffle oil and chopped fresh parsley are all good additions to this basic Mac 'n' Cheese recipe.*

# PARMESAN PORK SCHNITZEL WITH CAPER DRESSING

There are very few more satisfying things to eat than breaded meat fried in butter, especially when there's Parmesan in the breadcrumbs. This classic schnitzel can be devoured with a side of boiled new potatoes or stuffed into a bread roll. Once upon a time, you may not have let a caper near your pizza, nevermind make a dressing out of them. Unleash a new adventurous spirit in your taste buds!

## SERVES 2

400g **pork tenderloin**

6 tbsp **plain flour**

1 **egg**, beaten

100g fresh **breadcrumbs**

3 tbsp grated **Parmesan cheese**

2 tbsp **oil**

Knob of **butter**

2 x crusty **bread rolls**, to serve

**Lettuce** leaves, to serve

**Gherkins**, to serve

**Salt** and **pepper**

## FOR THE DRESSING

1 tbsp **red wine vinegar**

1 tsp **Dijon mustard**

4 tbsp **olive oil**

2 tbsp **capers**, drained

1 **gherkin**, drained and finely diced

2 tbsp freshly chopped **parsley**

**Make** the dressing first: put all of the ingredients together in a bowl and whisk with a fork. Taste for seasoning before leaving to one side while you tackle the schnitzel.

**Slice** the pork tenderloin in half so that you are left with two short but thick pieces of pork. Taking one piece at a time, place the meat on a chopping board. Tear off a piece of cling film roughly 20cm long and lay it over the top of the meat. Now pick a weapon; a blunt, reasonably heavy implement is what you're after – a rolling pin works best, but this can also be done with the base of a saucepan.

**Begin** bashing the piece of meat, lightly at first, and then more heavily as you become accustomed to the weight of your weapon. What you are aiming for is a piece of meat about 5mm thick. You may find on your first attempt that you get carried away and bash a hole in the meat; don't worry, the meat will ultimately be breadcrumbed.

**Once** you have reached the required thickness, carefully peel the meat off the board and leave to one side while you repeat the process with the second chunk of pork.

**By** now you should have a lovely dressing steeping on the side and two prepped pieces of pork. Take out three clean plates. Pour the flour onto the first plate and season well with salt and pepper. Pour the beaten egg onto the second, and finally tumble the breadcrumbs and the Parmesan onto the third. Using a fork, lightly mix the Parmesan into the breadcrumbs. You are about to become a schnitzel assembly line.

- **Season** both pieces of pork. Take the first one and place it in the flour, making sure that it is well coated. Pick it up in your hands and tap lightly to remove any excess flour. Next, dip the floured meat into the egg and swish around so there is a nice layer of egg all over. Finally, remove from the egg and allow any excess egg to drip off, before laying the pork in the crumbs. Press down gently to make sure the meat is well covered with the crumbs, before moving the meat to a clean plate. Voila! Breadcrumbed pork! Repeat the process with the second piece of meat.

- **Heat** the oil and butter in a large frying pan over a medium to high heat until gently bubbling. Carefully lay your schnitzel in a single layer in the frying pan and cook for 4 minutes on one side before gently turning and frying for a further 4 minutes on the other. Remove the beautifully browned meat to kitchen paper to drain off any excess fat.

- **Slice** your bread roll and stuff it with a few lettuce leaves. Layer on the schnitzel and lovingly spoon over your new favourite caper dressing. Give yourself a massive pat on the back and get stuck in.

# PORK CHOPS WITH EASY GRAVY

Rather than going into how to make a delicious sage and onion stuffing, and how to turn cooking juices into a gravy, we've taken a shortcut using Messrs Paxo and Bisto. It's the culinary equivalent of photocopying an entire year's worth of notes from somebody who actually turned up to lectures . . . and then getting an 'A' in the exams. So bad, but so good.

**SERVES 4**

7 tbsp **Paxo sage and onion stuffing**

4 **pork chops**, with or without the bone in

2 tbsp **oil**

1 head of **broccoli**, florets only

Splash of **red wine**

1 dried **bay leaf**

4 tsp **Bisto granules**

Boiled **new potatoes**, to serve

**Preheat** the oven to 190°C (gas mark 5).

**Empty** the dried stuffing into a bowl and add 200ml boiling water. Mix together with a spoon, then leave for 10 minutes. After this time you should find you have a loose stuffing mix.

**Take** each pork chop in turn and, using a spoon, spread the stuffing onto one side. Try to coat evenly and press down to keep it in place.

**Heat** the oil in a frying pan over a medium to high heat. Once it is hot, add the pork chops, stuffing side down. Fry, without turning, for 4 minutes. Flip each chop and continue to fry for a further 4 minutes. Place the browned chops on a baking tray and transfer to the preheated oven to bake for 15 minutes. Remove the chops from the oven and leave to rest for 5 minutes. Just enough time to make your gravy.

**Bring** a large saucepan of water to boiling point. Add the broccoli and cook for 4 minutes until just tender. Carefully spoon the florets from the water into a waiting bowl and leave to one side. Don't drain away the cooking liquid; instead, drain off only some of it so that you are left with what looks like the right amount for two people to have gravy (about 300ml).

**Place** the broccoli water in the saucepan back over a high heat and add the splash of red wine and the bay leaf. Bring to the boil and allow to simmer for 30 seconds before adding enough Bisto granules to thicken to a gravy.

**Serve** your delicious cheat's meal of stuffing-topped pork chops with Pea and Leek Fricassee (see page opposite), boiled new potatoes and gravy – and not even a hint of shame.

# PEA AND LEEK FRICASSEE

When peas are combined with butter and stock they become a sublime and quite substantial dish that can be served with almost any cooked meat – they go especially well with the Pork Chops with Easy Gravy on the opposite page.

**SERVES 4**

1 tbsp **oil**

Generous knob of **butter**

2 **leeks**, trimmed, washed and sliced into thin rounds

100ml **chicken** or **vegetable stock**

250g **frozen peas**

**Heat** the oil and butter in a saucepan over a medium to high heat. Once it is lightly bubbling, add the sliced leek. Fry for 3–4 minutes, stirring occasionally, until the leek has softened a little.

**Tumble** in the peas and pour in the stock. Bring everything to the boil, stirring a couple of times. Simmer for 1 minute.

**Serve** the vegetables with the Pork Chops and Easy Gravy on the opposite page or any other meat main you like.

# ROAST CHICKEN AND GRAVY

Nothing beats a roast chicken. You can dish it up with any of the roast vegetables on page 102 and if you are feeling flush, try to buy the best-quality, chicken you can afford. Our favourite is the corn-fed, free-range variety for better flavour and succulence.

## SERVES 4

1.5 kg **whole chicken**, string removed

Few drizzles of **olive oil**

500ml **chicken stock**

100ml **white wine** or 75ml **dry sherry**

1 dried **bay leaf**

3 tbsp **plain flour**

**Salt** and **pepper**

- **Preheat** the oven to 190°C (gas mark 5).

- **Place** the chicken upside down on a lightly oiled, heavy-based roasting tray – yes, that's right, upside down. Drizzle over a little olive oil and then season well with salt and pepper. Roast in the preheated oven for 45 minutes.

- **After** this time, remove the tray from the oven and carefully turn the bird the right way up. This is best done by putting a fork or the handle of a wooden spoon into the cavity of the bird, then holding it lightly at the other end and carefully flipping it over. Season the breast side with salt and pepper, then return the chickens to the oven.

- **After** another 30 minutes, remove the chicken from the oven, checking it is done by inserting a sharp knife into the underside of the leg in its thickest part. If the juices run clear without a hint of pinkness then it is cooked. Carefully transfer the chicken to a plate. Cover with foil and leave in a warm place to rest while you make the gravy.

- **Pour** the chicken stock and white wine (or sherry) into a saucepan and add the bay leaf. Bring to the boil, then simmer for 2 minutes. Turn off the heat and leave to one side.

- **Place** the roasting tray (that the chicken was cooked in) over a medium to high heat (see Tip) and sprinkle over the flour. Using a wooden spoon, quickly mix the flour into the fat and oil in the pan. Scrape any of the caramelised chicken bits from the base of the pan too. Continue to stir and cook for 2 minutes.

- **Turn** off the heat and pour in a quarter of your stock mix. Stir well to incorporate with the flour. There may be a few lumps, but try to smooth these out with your spoon or a fork. Pour in

the remaining stock and mix again. Turn the heat back on and
bring the gravy up to the boil, stirring frequently.

**Leave** the gravy to simmer for 2 minutes and then transfer
into a clean saucepan. Pour any juices that may have gathered
underneath the cooked chicken on the plate into the pan and
stir to mix. Your gravy is now ready to be reheated as needed
and served with the perfect roast chicken.

**Tip:** *If you don't have a roasting tray that can be used*
*directly on a hob just scrape all of the contents of the tray*
*into a clean saucepan.*

# THE PERFECT ROAST DINNER

There's a reason that your mum normally sits down to her Sunday roast a little red-cheeked and flustered; it's because it is not the easiest of meals to bring together. Even the best-planned Sunday roast demands a certain level of oven juggling and furious stirring as it approaches its delicious finale. It is, however, all worth it; from the cauliflower cheese to the gravy, there is no stronger call to the table, no better reason to enjoy each other's company, than the roast you have so lovingly prepared. You can mix-and-match the following recipes as you like – we won't think any less of you.

## ROAST BEEF WITH YORKSHIRE PUDDINGS AND GRAVY

There's a very specific time of year when, just for a few days, you feel like a lottery winner (loan time). It's in this short time when the roast beef dinner hits the agenda. Let's push the (gravy) boat out.

**SERVES 6**

2 kg piece of boneless **rolled beef rib** at room temperature

Drizzle of **oil**

3 tbsp **plain flour**

Splash of **red wine** (optional)

500ml **beef stock**

**Salt** and **pepper**

FOR THE YORKSHIRE PUDDINGS (MAKES 10)

200g **plain flour**

6 **eggs**

150ml **milk**

150ml **water**

Splash of **white vinegar**

10 tbsp **vegetable oil**

**Preheat** the oven to 220°C (gas mark 7).

**Place** your meat on a roasting tray. Drizzle with olive oil and season generously with salt and pepper.

**Roast** the meat in the preheated oven for 15 minutes, then reduce the temperature to 170°C (gas mark 3) and continue to cook for 15 minutes for every 500g to achieve a medium-rare meat. Add an extra 15 minutes to the whole cooking time for medium and an extra 30 minutes for well done (sacrilege).

**While** the meat is cooking, prepare your Yorkshire pudding batter. Tip the flour into a bowl and add the eggs, water, milk and a splash of vinegar. Whisk the whole lot together until you have a smooth batter. Pour the mixture into a jug and set aside until later.

**Once** cooked to your liking, remove the meat from the roasting tray and wrap in foil. Place the wrapped meat somewhere warm (the grill part above the main oven is convenient) to rest for at least 20 minutes.

- **Meanwhile,** increase the oven temperature to 200°C (gas mark 6). Pour a tablespoon of vegetable oil into 10 holes of a muffin tray or 10 individual pudding moulds. Place in the preheated oven and heat for at least 10 minutes.

- **Once** the oil has heated, pour the Yorkshire pudding batter equally into the 10 muffin tray holes or individual moulds. The batter should fry and sizzle almost instantly. Place the tray back in the oven and cook for 20 minutes without opening the oven door.

- **Make** your gravy while the meat is resting and the puddings are cooking. If your roasting tray is hob-proof, place it directly over a medium heat. If not, pour and scrape as much of the roasting tray contents as possible into a clean saucepan and place that over a medium heat. Sprinkle in the flour and stir well with a wooden spoon so that the fat absorbs all of it. Continue to stir and cook for 2 minutes before removing the tray from the heat and pouring in the red wine (if using) – stir until the flour and fat mix has absorbed it. Follow the wine with a quarter of the stock. Once that has been absorbed, add a further quarter and stir in. Place the pan back over the heat and pour in the remaining stock, then stir and bring to the boil. Take the pan off the heat. The gravy can be reheated when needed.

- **Check** your rested meat. If any juices have collected in the tin foil, then pour this into your gravy.

- **Carve** your meat, reheat your gravy if necessary and serve alongside piping-hot, statuesque Yorkshire puddings.

# CAULIFLOWER CHEESE

Cauliflower is one of those vegetables that remind you of school dinners. However, once it is coated with delicious cheese sauce and baked, something magical happens, for what emerges from the oven is one of the most delicious side dishes known to man.

**SERVES 6**

1 **cauliflower**

1 quantity of **Cheese Sauce** (see pages 30–31)

- **Preheat** the oven to 200°C (gas mark 6).

- **Cut** the cauliflower into florets – turn it upside down on your chopping board, use a small sharp knife to remove the core and leaves, then break off the florets.

- **Bring** a large saucepan of salted water to the boil and add the cauliflower florets. Simmer for 8 minutes before draining through a colander and running under cold water to cool quickly.

- **Tumble** the cooked florets into the prepared cheese sauce and fold so that all the cauliflower is coated. Tip into an ovenproof dish and bake in the preheated oven for 15–20 minutes until golden and bubbling.

# ROAST VEG

No traditional roast dinner is complete without a medley of roasted vegetables, and ours is no different. We have included some onions to add just a hint of sweetness.

**SERVES 6**

6 **carrots**, peeled and chopped into batons

4 **parsnips**, peeled and chopped into batons

2 large **red onions**, peeled and chopped into wedges

4 tbsp **olive oil**

**Salt** and **pepper**

- **Preheat** the oven to 190°C (gas mark 5).

- **Place** all the vegetables on a baking tray, drizzle with the olive oil and season generously with salt and pepper. Mix together with your hands until all the vegetables are evenly coated with the oil.

- **Place** the tray in the oven and roast for 50 minutes, turning the veg during the cooking time.

- **Tip:** *Remember to chop all the vegetables to roughly the same size to ensure even cooking.*

# CARROT AND SWEDE MASH

Carrots and swede are not only tasty, they also display the longevity of a fossil – especially the swede, which can be kept in the fridge or in a cool place for as long as . . . well, we don't know, because we've never seen one go off!

**SERVES 6**

1 **swede**, peeled and roughly chopped into small cubes

4 **carrots**, roughly chopped into small cubes

Generous knob of **butter**

**Salt** and **pepper**

**Place** the prepared vegetables in a large saucepan and cover generously with water. Set the pan over a high heat and bring to the boil before reducing to a simmer and cooking for 12–15 minutes – until the carrots and swede are both tender when poked with a fork.

**Drain** the vegetables through a colander and tumble back into the pan they were cooked in. Add the butter and season well with salt and pepper.

**Using** a potato masher, crush the vegetables together. Don't do this too vigorously – you are not looking for a smooth mash; rather something with a bit of texture.

**Serve** this dish as part of any kind of roast dinner or with almost any meat dish.

# COTTAGE PIE

This is a dish for all occasions. Whether it's the girls coming over before heading to the union or you are meeting your new boyfriend's or girlfriend's parents for the first time and wanting a dish that says 'I'm a keeper', cottage pie is the one for you.

## SERVES 6

3 tbsp **oil**

1 **onion**, peeled and grated

2 **carrots**, peeled and grated

800g **minced beef**

1 tbsp **plain flour**

300ml **beef stock**

5 tbsp **Worcestershire sauce**

200g **frozen peas**

2 portions of **Mashed Potato** (see page 19)

**Salt** and **pepper**

**Preheat** the oven to 200°C (gas mark 6).

**Heat** the oil in a large saucepan or frying pan over a medium to high heat. Once the oil is hot, add the grated vegetables and cook for 5 minutes, stirring regularly, until they have softened.

**Increase** the heat to maximum. Once there is a good sizzle, add the minced beef and stir a little to break up the meat. Fry the meat for 3–5 minutes, trying not to stir too often. Sprinkle in the flour and stir to incorporate. Fry for a further minute.

**Remove** the pan from the heat and pour in the stock and Worcestershire sauce, stirring well to incorporate. Place the pan back on the heat and reduce the heat to medium. Let the mixture simmer for a couple of minutes before pouring in the peas and adding the seasoning to taste. Mix together and turn off the heat.

**Pour** the cooked mixture into an ovenproof dish and leave to cool to room temperature while you make your mashed potato according to the instructions on page 19.

**While** the potato is still warm, top the cooled mixture with the mash. Bake in the preheated oven for 30 minutes until golden on top and bubbling around the sides. Let the dish stand for at least 5 minutes before serving up heaps of steaming cottage pie to a suitably impressed audience.

**Tip:** *You can prepare the cottage pie up to the point when it is ready to go in the oven and then cover the dish and place it in the fridge for the next day. Remove the dish from the fridge an hour before cooking, then bake in a preheated oven for 30–40 minutes.*

# MUSHROOM AND HERB FILO ROLLS

Vegetarian meals always seem to try and replicate their meaty counterparts, making vegetarianism seem like a lesser substitute. Here's a recipe that stares into the face of meat and refuses to be put down. Behold the Mushroom and Herb Filo Roll, so satisfying that even the most ardent carnivore may not even notice the lack of meat until they have finished licking their plate.

## SERVES 4

50g **butter**, plus 80g melted

1 **onion**, peeled and finely diced

2 fresh **thyme** sprigs

250g assorted **mushrooms**, chopped

300g fresh **bread**, roughly grated or ready-packed fresh **breadcrumbs** (avoid dried breadcrumbs)

200g **mixed nuts**, roughly chopped

2 tbsp freshly chopped **sage**

2 tbsp freshly chopped **parsley** (optional)

1 **egg**

1 x 270g packet of **filo pastry sheets** (a minimum of 6 A4-size pieces)

1 tbsp **sesame seeds** (optional)

**Salt** and **pepper**

**Preheat** the oven to 190°C (gas mark 5).

**Melt** the 50g butter in a large saucepan over a medium to high heat. Once melted and bubbling, add the onion and thyme. Cook for 6–8 minutes, until the onions are soft but not coloured. Add the mushrooms and fry with the onions for 5 minutes, until they are just beginning to soften.

**Remove** the pan from the heat and stir in the breadcrumbs. They should absorb the butter and almost melt in the pan. Add the mixed nuts, some salt and pepper, the sage and parsley (if using). Stir to mix everything together well. Add the egg and quickly stir again so that it doesn't cook on the warm mixture. Leave to one side.

**Remove** the filo from the packet. You are ultimately looking for sheets roughly the size of an A4 piece of paper – this may take a little trimming. Take one piece of filo and brush with the melted butter. Lay another sheet of filo on top of this – the filo sheets should stick satisfyingly to one another.

**Lay** the 2-ply sheet in front of you so that it is sitting portrait style. Take a quarter of your nut mixture and mound it at the edge closest to you, leaving a 4cm border on three sides and the remaining length of filo in front. Fold the two long sides over the stuffing to encase it at the edges. Now lift the edge closest to you and roll the mixture into a sausage shape. Once the mixture has been rolled over three times, trim any excess pastry. Place your sausage-shaped filo roll on a baking tray, brush with more melted butter and sprinkle with a few sesame seeds.

**Repeat** the process with the remaining pastry and mixture to make 4 filo rolls. Place the tray in the oven and bake for 30 minutes or until the pastry is golden. Serve your filo rolls to vegetarians and carnivores alike.

# NIFTY LUNCHES

Whether it's for a friend's barbecue on a beautiful sunny Saturday or a slightly less fun lecture-filled day, you can save money and time by preparing your own lunch.

In this chapter we move from the basics of delicious sandwich fillings through to the more complicated but massively impressive Sausage and Red Pepper Rolls.

# SPANISH OMELETTE

There is no doubt about it, this is one of the most delicious dishes on the planet. Eggs, spuds and onions combine in beautiful synergetic harmony. Master this dish and you will always have a very satisfying plate of food at your fingertips.

**SERVES 2**

6 tbsp **olive oil**

1 large **onion**, peeled and finely sliced

1 large **potato**, peeled and roughly chopped into small chunks

6 **eggs**

**Rocket leaves**, to garnish

**Salt** and **pepper**

**Heat** half the oil in a non-stick frying pan about 20cm in diameter over a medium heat. Once hot, add the sliced onion and fry for about 10 minutes until meltingly soft.

**Meanwhile**, bring a large saucepan of salted water to the boil. Once boiling, tumble in the chunks of potato and boil for about 8 minutes until cooked all the way through, but still holding their shape. This can be tested by pushing a fork into a chunk of potato – when it's ready the fork should pierce the potato easily. Drain the potato chunks through a colander and leave to dry off a little in the colander.

**Once** the onion is cooked, increase the heat to maximum, and when the pan is hot add the cooked potato. Fry the potato and onion together, stirring occasionally, for 2–3 minutes.

**Crack** the eggs into a bowl, season well with salt and pepper and whisk thoroughly.

**Pour** the remaining oil into the frying pan and reduce the heat to medium. Slowly pour in the beaten egg mixture. It will be quite cramped in the pan, so you may need to use a wooden spoon to work some of the egg in. When all of the egg mixture is in the pan, carefully stir, ensuring that you scrape across the base. The egg should be coming together a little like scrambled egg. After about 1 minute of stirring and frying there should be a reasonable amount of cooked egg, topped with a lot of raw egg. At this point, leave to cook without stirring for 2 minutes to create a base.

**The** next bit takes a little bravery: place a large, upturned plate over the frying pan so that the base is pointing up at you. Place one hand on the base of the plate and grip the frying pan handle with the other. In one swift and confident motion, flip the omelette onto the plate. You should now be looking at a gloriously golden base.

**Add** a drizzle more olive oil to the pan and once it is hot, gently slide your omelette back in so that the raw side is now on the base. You can now breathe. Fry for a further 5 minutes like this over a medium to high heat.

**Slip** your glorious Spanish Omelette onto a chopping board and let it sit for a couple of minutes before dividing it up into portions, garnishing with rocket leaves and regaling your peers with the story of your egg-flipping heroics. Olé!

**Tip:** *If you do not feel confident enough to flip the omelette, then simply put the pan under a hot grill to finish cooking.*

**Variation:** *Like all good recipes, this one is open to variations. As long as you use the three main ingredients, you can add all sorts of extras, such as grated courgette, baby spinach, roast chicken, chorizo or cheese.*

# BUTTERNUT SQUASH AND GOAT'S CHEESE RISOTTO

Here's a great dish full of autumnal colours and flavours. This is one of those meals that a bog-standard restaurant will charge you a small fortune for, and serve you a bog-standard version. Cook this recipe and there will be nothing bog-standard about the results. It can be eaten on its own or with a grilled pork chop to create a dish worthy of a place on any table.

## SERVES 4

3 tbsp **olive oil**

Small knob of **butter**

1 small **onion**, peeled and finely diced

1 fresh **thyme** sprig

250g **risotto rice**

½ medium **butternut squash**, peeled and grated

½ glass of **white wine** (optional)

1.25 litres hot **chicken** or **vegetable stock**

100g **frozen peas**

½ x 125g pack of **soft goat's cheese**

Generous grating of **Parmesan cheese**

**Salt** and **pepper**

**Heat** the oil and butter in a large saucepan over a medium to high heat. Once bubbling, add the onion. Cook for about 5 minutes, stirring regularly, until the onion has softened and is starting to take on a little colour. Add the thyme sprig and cook for a further minute. Turn up the heat to maximum.

**Add** the rice and the grated butternut squash to the pan, and stir while frying for 2–3 minutes. Pour in the white wine (if using) and let it bubble and reduce by half. Reduce the heat a little before pouring in a ladle or two of the hot stock. Keep stirring to mix thoroughly. It should start to bubble away and release some of the starch from the rice immediately.

**Continue** the process of adding small amounts of hot stock to the risotto and stirring well until all of the stock is absorbed – this should take about 20 minutes. You should now be looking at a very inviting dish of creamy, just-cooked risotto rice.

**Reduce** the heat to low and tip in the peas, stir and leave to bubble for 1 minute before adding both the cheeses. Stir until well combined. You should notice your risotto becoming luxurious from the cheeses. Turn off the heat, check for seasoning and serve immediately.

**Tip:** *This dish freezes very well and can be reheated either in the microwave, or from frozen in a pan over a medium heat – just keep an eye on it and make sure that you let it boil for at least a minute before serving.*

# FANCY BLUE CHEESE MUSHROOMS ON TOAST

This is a classic gastropub-style starter, and it's too good and too cheap for us not to include. It's worth pushing the boat out a little on the bread to accompany this dish. Save the sliced white for the sausage sandwich and blow the budget on a bloomer.

## SERVES 4

3 tbsp **butter**

2 **garlic** cloves, peeled and finely chopped

2 x 300g packs of **mushrooms**, cleaned and chopped in half

½ glass of **white wine**

300ml **double cream**

1 x 200g block of **blue cheese** (Roquefort or Stilton), rind removed, broken into chunks

**Bread** and **butter**, to serve

Small bunch of fresh **parsley**, chopped (optional)

**Melt** the butter in a large frying pan over a medium to high heat. Once bubbling, add the garlic and fry for 1 minute. Add the mushrooms and fry for 4 minutes, stirring occasionally so that they pick up a little colour.

**Increase** the heat to maximum and pour in the white wine. Let it reduce by half before turning the heat down to medium and adding the cream. Wait a little for the cream to heat through, then, while stirring regularly, drop in the blue cheese, piece by piece. It should all begin to melt and become part of a deliciously creamy sauce. Do not let it come up to the boil.

**Leave** the sauce to sit while you toast your bread and butter it. Serve generous amounts of the mushroom sauce, scattered with chopped parsley (if using), over toasted slices of hot buttered bread.

*Tip: The mushroom sauce in this recipe can be cooled and used as an alternative filling for the Unbelievably Easy Ham and Cheese Pasty (see pages 124–125).*

# PRAWN, FETA AND QUINOA SALAD

Quinoa is one of those achingly fashionable ancient grains that has been rediscovered, repackaged and re-marketed as the elixir of all healthy living — and for good reason. Not only is it a tasty grain, but it is also packed full of protein that will keep you fuller for longer. Try this recipe before you sit your final exams and revel in the slow-release energy that will help you concentrate all the way to a first-class degree.

## SERVES 4

400g **quinoa**

½ **cucumber**, deseeded and chopped into small pieces

½ jar of roasted **red peppers**, drained and chopped

2 **spring onions**, trimmed and finely sliced

8 tbsp **olive oil**

100g **feta** cheese

1 tbsp dried **oregano**

1 **red chilli**, deseeded and finely chopped

16 raw **king prawns**

Fresh **mint** and **lemon**, to serve (optional)

**Salt** and **pepper**

**Fill** a large saucepan with salted water and bring to boiling point. Add the quinoa and cook according to the packet instructions (or for about 10 minutes). Drain the quinoa through a sieve, then run under cold water to instantly cool.

**Tip** the drained and cooled quinoa into a large bowl and add the cucumber, chopped red peppers, spring onions, 2 tablespoons of the olive oil and some salt and pepper. Crumble the feta over the quinoa and mix all the ingredients together. Place your salad to one side while you cook the prawns.

**Pour** 4 tablespoons of the olive oil into a bowl. Sprinkle over the dried oregano before adding the chopped red chilli. Mix well and leave to one side.

**Heat** the remaining olive oil in a large frying pan over a high heat. Once hot, add the prawns and fry without stirring for 2 minutes. Turn the prawns and fry for a further 2 minutes. Cooking times may vary depending on the size of your prawns, but try not to overcook the prawns.

**Once** your prawns have turned a coral colour and are lightly golden in places, tip them straight into the oregano oil and turn a couple of times to pick up some of the flavoured oil.

**Serve** your prawns alongside the quinoa salad, sprinkled with fresh mint and a squeeze of lemon juice (if using).

**Variation:** *For a vegetarian take, simply substitute the prawns with sliced and fried halloumi slices.*

# TUNA AND COURGETTE FRITTERS

Throughout student halls, canteens and bars across the country, tuna mayonnaise is slathered over white bread and dolloped atop baked potatoes – it has become the fuel of our student nation. Well, guess what! There is another way of preparing tinned tuna, and it does go with another vegetable other than sweetcorn. Try this recipe, and you may never find yourself reaching for the mayonnaise again.

**MAKES 12**

1 x 160g tin of **tuna**

1 **courgette**, grated

75g **self-raising flour**

1 **egg**

**Oil**, to shallow fry

Light **soy sauce**, to serve

**Salt** and **pepper**

**Drain** the tuna and fork it into a bowl, breaking up the chunks. Add the grated courgette, self-raising flour and egg and season with a good amount of salt and black pepper.

**Using** your fork, mix all the ingredients together well until you achieve a slightly runny batter. If necessary, add just a little water at a time to attain a dropping consistency – it should be the thickness of double cream or custard.

**Pour** enough oil into a frying pan to completely cover the base and heat over a medium to high heat. When hot, use a couple of tablespoons to drop spoonfuls of batter into the pan. It is by no means necessary to make perfect circles, but a consistent size and shape will help you judge cooking times.

**Once** the fritters have fried for 2–3 minutes on one side, flip them over. The cooked side should be lightly browned. If it isn't, don't attempt to flip back, instead give it a little longer on the side it is on, before flipping later to finish.

**If** all has gone to plan, then continue to cook for 2–3 minutes before removing from the pan and placing on kitchen paper to absorb any excess oil.

**Keep** the cooked fritters in a warm place (an oven set on a low heat is perfect) while you repeat the process with the remaining batter. Try not to eat as you are going, although this is easier said than done.

**Serve** the fritters with a drizzle of soy sauce for a very satisfying lunch.

# SAUSAGE AND RED PEPPER ROLLS

We all know about sausage rolls — there are fewer more satisfying savoury snacks available. However, we think it's time to give the humble roll a little European makeover. So here is our Spanish take on the very English sausage roll.

**MAKES 4**

4 **sausages**

75g **chorizo sausage**, diced

3–4 **roasted red peppers** from a jar, drained and chopped into small pieces

**Flour**, for dusting

1 x 500g pack of **puff pastry**

1 **egg**, beaten

**Preheat** the oven to 190°C (gas mark 5).

**All** you want from your sausages is the meat inside the case. Therefore gently squeeze the sausage, and the meat should begin to appear from one of the ends. Empty all of the sausage meat into a large bowl.

**Add** the diced chorizo and the chopped red peppers. Mix the ingredients thoroughly so they are fully combined.

**Dust** a clean surface with a little flour. Roll out the block of pastry into a large square about ½cm thick. Using a sharp knife, cut the pastry into 4 smaller squares of equal size. Trim the edges to make neat squares.

**Divide** your sausage mixture into 4 portions. Taking one of your portions at a time, spread it lengthways along the middle of a pastry square, making sure you leave a generous border all the way around.

**Brush** the edge of the pastry with a little beaten egg before folding the pastry widthways over the sausage meat. Lightly press the edges together with the back of a fork to both seal the pastry and to create a pattern, before brushing all over with beaten egg. Finally, slash the top of the pastry in three or four places using a sharp knife (this will let the steam escape during cooking). Place the roll on a baking tray or a tray lined with baking parchment. Repeat the process with the remaining sausage mixture and pastry.

**Bake** the rolls in the preheated oven for 30 minutes until golden and risen. Leave the rolls to cool on a wire rack for 5 minutes. Eat either hot or cold.

# THE INVINCIBLE SANDWICH

OK, we've done it. Just when you thought that our recipes couldn't be any simpler, here we are with a section on sandwiches. Seriously, if you want to save money, you will soon realise that the £2.50 a day you are shelling out for a limp and unsatisfactory sandwich from the canteen adds up to a large chunk of your budget. Take the next few recipes, not as patronisingly simple, but as a nudge in the right direction. All the below sandwich fillings will make enough to feed two very greedy mouths.

## PRAWN COCKTAIL

3 tbsp **mayonnaise**

2 tbsp **tomato ketchup**

Dash of **Tabasco sauce** (optional)

1 x 200g pack of ready-cooked and peeled **prawns**

4 slices of buttered **bread**

**Salt** and **pepper**

**Mix** the mayonnaise and ketchup together in a bowl. Add a dash of Tabasco (if using) and mix again.

**Open** the pack of prawns and tip them into the sauce. Mix until the prawns are coated, then taste and season.

**Serve** directly into mouth from bowl, or load up some buttered bread and serve with a little salad on the side.

## TUNA MAYONNAISE

1 x 250g tin of **tuna**

2 tbsp **mayonnaise**

½ tbsp **tomato ketchup**

4 slices of buttered **bread**

1 **cucumber**, sliced (optional)

**Salt** and **pepper**

**Drain** and flake the tuna into a bowl using a fork to break up some of the bigger chunks.

**Add** the mayonnaise, tomato ketchup, a little salt and a generous amount of black pepper. Mix well until all of the ingredients are well incorporated.

**Spread** generously over your sliced bread and add a few slices of cucumber (if using).

# EASY CORONATION CHICKEN

2 tbsp **mayonnaise**

2 tsp **curry paste**

1 tbsp **mango chutney**

2 **cooked chicken breasts**, sliced into 1cm pieces

4 slices of **bread**

**Iceberg lettuce**, shredded

1 **tomato**, sliced

**Put** the mayonnaise, curry paste and mango chutney in a bowl and mix well to combine all the ingredients.

**Add** the chicken pieces to the bowl and fold gently through the sauce. Spread the filling over your sliced bread, along with a couple of tomato slices and shredded iceberg lettuce to add a little crunch.

**Chop** your sandwiches into triangles, doff your cap, drop a knee and hum the national anthem as you munch on your delicious sandwiches.

*Tip: Almost anything that can be put in a sandwich can also be rolled up in a warmed tortilla. Don't be shy about using things like leftover mince as a sandwich filler. Our rule: if you can trap it between two slices of bread, then it's a genuine sandwich filling.*

# UNBELIEVABLY EASY HAM AND CHEESE PASTY

Cook this recipe as your first foray into baking and we guarantee you will find a queue of beautiful-looking men and women at your door asking for your family baking tips. Our advice: play it cool, answer mysteriously and make sure you hide this book.

**MAKES 4**

**Flour**, for dusting

1 x 500g pack of **puff pastry**, fridge cold

100g **thick-cut ham**, diced

150g **Cheddar cheese**, grated

4 **spring onions**

1 **egg**, beaten

**Preheat** the oven to 200°C (gas mark 6).

**Dust** a clean surface with a generous amount of flour and place your block of pastry on it. Using a rolling pin, begin to roll out the pastry. Because it is cold this may be quite hard work at first. You are aiming for a sheet about ½cm thick and large enough to cut 4 saucer-size discs from it.

**Once** you have rolled out your pastry, gently lay a saucer about 15cm in diameter on the pastry. Position it to get the best use out of the pastry – not straight in the middle, but in one of the corners. Carefully cut around the saucer with a sharp knife. Repeat this three times, then discard the remaining pastry. You should now have 4 discs of pastry.

**Now** for the filling: place the ham and cheese in a bowl. Chop off the tips with the stringy bits from each spring onion and discard. Finely slice the spring onions and add to the bowl with the ham and cheese. Use your hands to mix thoroughly.

**Take** one of your pastry circles and place a quarter of the ham and cheese mixture right in the middle of the circle, ensuring that you leave at least a 2cm border around the edge. The mixture can be piled reasonably high. Dip your finger into the beaten egg and paint the edge of the pastry that you have left clear of filling. Wash your eggy finger.

**Fold** the pastry edge closest to you over the filling in the middle and push down to meet the pastry on the far side. The pastry edges should stick together. Some of the filling may have tried to escape during the folding process, so just carefully push it back in before sealing.

**Gently** press down the two edges of the pastry all the way round to create a semi-circular, pasty-shaped package. Use the back of a fork to press down on the edge to ensure the pastry is properly sealed – this will also give your pasty an attractive finish (secret family baking tip). Place the pasty on a non-stick baking tray while you repeat the process with the remaining pastry circles and ham and cheese filling.

**Once** you have 4 perfectly formed pasties, dip your finger back into the beaten egg and 'wash' the top of the pasties. Bake in the preheated oven for 20–25 minutes or until the pastry is golden and has risen nicely.

**Enjoy** the pasties piping hot from the oven or leave to cool down for a perfect hangover-busting savoury hit.

**Tip:** *The pasties can be frozen once they are ready to go in the oven – just wrap well in cling film or put in a freezer bag. The pasties should cook perfectly from frozen if you bake them in an oven preheated to 180°C (gas mark 4) for 40 minutes or until golden and the cheese is melting.*

# CROWD PLEASERS

People around campus have started to notice that you cook, and they're beginning to take an interest in the way that you prepare your food. Before long they're muttering to each other, 'I hear they're good, but they've never cooked for me.' When that happens, it's time to step it up. You need recipes that will have them licking their lips; recipes that support your fledgling culinary reputation. These are those recipes.

But that doesn't mean these recipes are excruciatingly difficult. There are dishes here for when you want minimum effort, maximum impact – deceptive dishes that will give that wow factor without causing you to break a sweat. C'mon, let's please the crowd! The following recipes are for just such occasions, as well as those times when you want to spoil your old friends, or impress new ones.

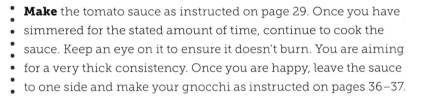

# GNOCCHI with TOMATO SAUCE AND RICOTTA

**Delicious, classy and simple. Nuff said.**

## SERVES 4

1 portion of **Simple Tomato Sauce** (see page 29)

1 portion of **Gnocchi** (see pages 36–37)

100g **ricotta cheese**

Small bunch of fresh **basil**, leaves only

**Salt** and **pepper**

**Make** the tomato sauce as instructed on page 29. Once you have simmered for the stated amount of time, continue to cook the sauce. Keep an eye on it to ensure it doesn't burn. You are aiming for a very thick consistency. Once you are happy, leave the sauce to one side and make your gnocchi as instructed on pages 36–37.

**Place** the boiled gnocchi into the reduced sauce and lightly mix. Divide the gnocchi and sauce between two plates and crumble over the ricotta cheese before topping with basil leaves and seasoning with salt and pepper.

**Variations:** *Try adding fried mushrooms or chorizo to the tomato base, or stir through a handful of spinach leaves just before serving for a healthy twist.*

# BAKED CAMEMBERT FOR TWO

This dish will clog your arteries, give you type 2 diabetes and probably a good dose of gout to top it all off. But who cares when food tastes this good?! For this recipe you need to buy a Camembert in a wooden box. They're available from all major supermarkets.

**SERVES 2**

1 x 250g **Camembert**, in a wooden box

1 **garlic** clove, peeled and finely sliced

1 **fresh rosemary** sprig, leaves only

**Toasted bread** and **cranberry sauce**, to serve

- **Preheat** the oven to 180°C (gas mark 4).

- **Take** the cheese out of the wooden box and remove any plastic packaging. Use a small, sharp knife to remove the rind from the top of the cheese (this doesn't have to be done perfectly), trying to retain as much of the cheese as possible. Place the cheese back in the wooden box with the rindless side facing up.

- **Using** the point of your knife, make small slits into the top of the cheese. Spike these slits with pieces of sliced garlic and leaves of rosemary.

- **Place** the box on a baking tray and bake in the oven for 15 minutes.

- **Serve** the meltingly gooey cheese straight from the oven alongside toasted bread for dipping into the centre. Add a little cranberry sauce on the side, if you like.

# SALMON DINNER IN A BAG

Fish is far and away the most intimidating ingredient for people to cook. Afraid of poisoning their friends or choking on a bone, cooks everywhere live their lives just eating battered fish from their local chip shop. It's time to man/woman up and cook some fish. And this is about as easy as fish cooking gets.

## SERVES 4

800g unpeeled **new potatoes**, sliced in half

2 heads of **broccoli**, florets only

4 skinless **salmon fillets**, weighing about 200g each

2 **garlic** cloves, peeled and finely chopped

4 tbsp **butter**, broken into a few small knobs

4 **spring onions**, white part only, trimmed and thinly sliced

8 tbsp either **chicken stock** or **white wine** or **water**

2 **lemons**, wedges for squeezing

**Salt** and **pepper**

**Preheat** the oven to 200°C (gas mark 6).

**Bring** a large saucepan of salted water to boiling point. Once boiling, tumble in the new potatoes and cook for about 12 minutes until just tender. About 3 minutes from the end of their cooking time, add the broccoli florets. Drain the whole lot through a colander and leave to one side.

**Roll** out two pieces of foil about 40cm long and lay one on top of the other. Place two salmon fillets, next to each other, about 10cm away from the edge closest to you in the middle of the foil rectangle. Scatter the garlic, butter and spring onion over the salmon fillets and season.

**Now** carefully place the boiled broccoli and potatoes on top of and around the salmon. Make sure you leave the border closest to you and at least 5cm either side of the salmon empty so you can form a parcel with the foil.

**Draw** the edge furthest away from you over the salmon and vegetables until it meets the edge closest to you. You should have now enveloped your salmon. Fold the joined edge over a couple of times to seal it. Do the same with one of the side edges. You should now have a parcel closed at two ends. Repeat with your second parcel and with the remaining fillets of salmon.

**Tipping** one of your parcels a little, pour in half the stock, wine or water. Now seal up the third and final edge to create a fully sealed tin foil 'bag'. Repeat with the second parcel. Carefully place the bags on a baking tray and cook in the preheated oven for 12 minutes. Remove from the oven and leave to sit for 2 minutes.

**Carefully** slice open the bags from the top and share the contents between plates. Squeeze over a little lemon juice before serving.

**Tip:** *Ensure that you ask your fishmonger (or supermarket fish counter tender) for skinless fillets, and try to choose fleshy-looking specimens of roughly the same dimensions so that they cook evenly.*

# SLOSHED MUSSELS

There's no need to travel to France to taste a truly authentic and delicious rendition of moules marinière; all you need is a pot with a lid. Mussels are your friend. They are one of the most delicious ingredients this wonderful planet we call Earth has to offer.

## SERVES 4

1.5 kg **mussels**

3 tbsp **oil**

3 banana **shallots**, peeled and finely chopped

3 **garlic** cloves, peeled and finely chopped

¾ glass of **white wine**

150ml **double cream**

Bunch of fresh **parsley**, chopped

Crusty **bread**, to serve

**Tip** the mussels into a large bowl and pull off any of the 'beards' you can see hanging from the sides. Run them under some cold water, while tumbling them around a little with your hands, before placing them in a bowl. Any mussels that are open at this point and do not close with a firm tap of the shell should be discarded. The mussels can now be left in the fridge like this for at least 4 hours, although when you do come to use them, give them a final run under the tap and repeat the tapping test for any that have opened.

**Heat** the oil in a large saucepan over a medium to high heat. Once hot, add the chopped shallots and garlic. Fry for 3 minutes before increasing the heat to maximum.

**When** the pan is very hot, tip in all of the mussels and stir to coat them with the shallot- and garlic-flavoured oil. Pour in the white wine and quickly clamp on a lid. Cook the mussels now for 6–8 minutes. During this time try not to remove the lid, but do shake the pan a couple of times to encourage even cooking.

**Remove** the lid and look inside the pan. You are aiming for all of the mussels to be open. If you spy quite a few that haven't opened then replace the lid, give the pan a shake and cook for a further 2 minutes. If there are just a couple that have not opened, then discard these unopened ones and carry on with the cooking.

**Use** a slotted spoon to place the mussels in four bowls. Place the saucepan back over a high heat and pour in the cream, bring to the boil and simmer for 2 minutes before pouring over the awaiting mussels. Scatter with generous amounts of chopped parsley

**Serve** to some lucky friends with crusty bread for dipping into the boozy sauce. Put a beret on and raise a glass of champagne to the heroes of the Bastille.

# CHICKEN AND BULGUR WHEAT

Bulgur wheat – you know it's good for you, and it's also unbelievably cheap, but there's the conundrum of how to prepare it. To realise the potential of humble bulgur wheat, all you have to do is cook this recipe. It uses saffron – admittedly a pricey ingredient – but it is this that makes the dish fit for kings and rajas.

**SERVES 4**

500ml **chicken stock**

About 8 strands of **saffron**

4 tbsp **oil**

6 **chicken** thighs, skin on and bone in

1 **red onion**, peeled and finely chopped

2 **celery** sticks, finely chopped

1 **cinnamon** stick, snapped in half

2 tbsp **tomato purée**

175g **bulgur wheat**

50g **raisins**

100g **feta cheese**

Handful of mixed freshly chopped **parsley** and **mint** (optional)

**Salt** and **pepper**

**Make** up your chicken stock however you normally do it. Assuming you are adding water to a cube or jelly, once you have poured the water in, add the saffron strands. Leave this to sit and infuse while you carry on with the rest of the dish.

**Heat** 2 tablespoons of the oil in a large saucepan over a medium to high heat. Season the chicken generously with salt and pepper. Once the oil is hot, add the chicken skin-side down (this may have to be done in batches) and fry for 3–4 minutes before turning to fry for a further 3–4 minutes. The flesh and skin should be nicely browned. Transfer the browned meat to a plate.

**Add** the remaining oil to the pan (if needed) and tip in the chopped red onion and celery. Fry over a medium to high heat for 3–4 minutes until the onion becomes soft. Turn down the heat if the onion starts to burn. Add the cinnamon stick and the tomato purée. Cook for a further 2 minutes, stirring frequently. Add the bulgur wheat and raisins and return the browned chicken thighs to the pan. Mix all the ingredients together for 2–3 minutes.

**Pour** in the infused stock and bring to the boil. Reduce the heat to a simmer, clamp on a lid and leave to cook for 15 minutes, stirring delicately every now and then. After this time, turn off the heat and leave to sit for a further 10 minutes, covered. The bulgur wheat should have absorbed the chicken stock and expanded. Remove the lid and 'rough up' the bulgur wheat with a fork.

**Serve** this Eastern delight with crumbled feta and fresh parsley and mint (if using) sprinkled on top.

# CHORIZO CHICKEN

Chorizo is one of the best ingredients ever made. Fact. Chicken is the best meat ever. Fact. Therefore this must be the best dish in the world. Hmm, maybe not quite, but it is pretty delicious.

## SERVES 6

4 tbsp **oil**

6 **chicken** thighs, skin on and bone in

1 **red onion**, peeled and finely diced

300g **chorizo**, chopped into small chunks

1 **red pepper**, deseeded and chopped

2 **garlic** cloves, peeled and finely chopped

1 x 400g tin of **chopped tomatoes**

2 tsp **caster sugar**

1 x 400g tin of **chickpeas**, drained and rinsed

375g **shredded kale**

**Salt** and **pepper**

**Heat** 2 tablespoons of the oil in a large saucepan over a medium to high heat. Season the chicken thighs with salt and pepper, and once the oil is hot, carefully place the thighs in the pan skin-side down. Fry without turning for about 5 minutes. You are looking to achieve a deep golden colour on the skin. Once you are happy with the colour, turn the chicken and continue to fry for a further 4 minutes, skin-side up.

**Remove** the chicken to a plate and roughly wipe out the pan with some kitchen paper before placing it back on the heat and pouring in the remaining oil. Once the oil is hot, add the red onion and chorizo and fry for about 4 minutes, stirring regularly, until the onion has softened and the chorizo has begun to release some of its delicious red oil. Add the red pepper and garlic and continue to stir-fry for a further 3 minutes.

**Put** the chicken back into the pan and mix to incorporate with all the other ingredients. Pour in the chopped tomatoes. Half fill the empty tin with water and tip that into the pan along with the sugar. Bring the stew up to the boil before reducing the heat to a simmer. Simmer for 10 minutes and then add the chickpeas.

**Continue** to simmer with the chickpeas for a further 5 minutes and then stir in the kale. Continue to cook for another 5 minutes.

**Your** ingredient relay is now over. Serve up your dish to friends, declaring it to be undoubtedly the best one-pot dish in the world.

# FAJITA PARTY

**Fajitas are top of the class when it comes to party food. And there are two main reasons why they are so well suited to such an occasion: 1) The DIY element helps break the ice and adds an element of fun. 2) Almost everything can be prepared in advance, which gives you time to bask in the compliments that are sure to come your way. The following recipes serves 10, but it can easily be scaled down for a lesser number. Go forth and enjoy!**

## SERVES 10

10 **chicken** breasts, sliced into thin strips

2 tbsp dried **oregano**

1 tbsp **ground cumin**

1 tbsp **smoked paprika**

5 **garlic** cloves, peeled and very finely diced

8 tbsp **olive oil**

## FOR THE GUACAMOLE

4 ripe **avocados**, cut in half, stoned and the flesh scooped out

2 **red chillies**, deseeded and finely diced

Juice of 2 **limes**

Small bunch of fresh **coriander**, chopped

**Salt** and **pepper**

- **Place** the chicken in a bowl and add the dried oregano, cumin, paprika, garlic and half the oil. Mix well and leave to marinate for a minimum of 1 hour, but preferably overnight.

- **Preheat** the oven to 110°C (gas mark ¼).

- **To** make the guacamole, put the avocado flesh in a bowl. Using the back of a fork, squash the avocado so that you are left with a bit of a mush and a few chunks. Add the rest of the ingredients, being generous with the salt and pepper, and mix well. Cover and leave at room temperature until ready to eat.

- **Make** the salsa. Put all the ingredients in a bowl, season generously with salt and pepper and mix well. Leave at room temperature until needed.

- **Cook** the marinated chicken in batches. Heat a third or half of the remaining oil (depending on how many batches you will have to do – we will presume a third) over a high heat in a large frying pan. Once hot, add a third of the chicken pieces and fry, stirring occasionally, for 5–6 minutes or until the chicken is cooked through. Tip the cooked mixture into an ovenproof dish, cover with foil and leave in the oven to keep warm while you continue cooking the rest of the chicken.

## FOR THE SALSA

5 ripe **tomatoes**, roughly chopped

2 tbsp **olive oil**

1 **red onion**, peeled and very finely diced

Juice of 2 **limes**

Small bunch of fresh **coriander**, chopped

**Salt** and **pepper**

## TO SERVE

24 flour **tortilla wraps**

250g **soured cream**

300g grated **Cheddar cheese**

1 **iceberg lettuce**, shredded

**When** you are ready to eat, warm the tortilla wraps in the oven along with the chicken. Put everything you have prepared on the table in separate bowls, along with a bowl each of soured cream, grated cheese and shredded lettuce, and encourage everyone to build their own wraps. Give yourself a large pat on the back and down an ice cold Corona to take the edge off all your hard work.

**Tip:** *Fajitas are the foodstuff that just keeps giving. If you have any leftovers then make yourself a delicious quesadilla. Simply heat a frying pan over a medium to high heat. Once hot, lay a tortilla in the pan and top with a good helping of cooked chicken and grated cheese. Place another tortilla on top and leave to cook like this for 3 minutes before carefully flipping and cooking the other way up for a further 4 minutes. Slide your quesadilla onto a chopping board and cut into hearty portions before topping with leftover guacamole or salsa. Yum!*

# SAUSAGE, SWEET POTATO AND PEPPER TRAY BAKE

Breakfast, dinner, lunch, sandwich, stew or casserole: the banger will constantly please you with its versatility. This super-easy meal is packed full of flavour, is reasonably good for you, and best of all there will be hardly any washing up to do because all you have to do is throw the ingredients into the tray and bake.

## SERVES 4

3 tbsp **olive oil**

2 **sweet potatoes**, washed and chopped into wedges

1 **red onion**, peeled and chopped into wedges

1 **red pepper**, deseeded and chopped into 2cm pieces

10 **sausages**

2 **fresh rosemary** sprigs, leaves only

1 **courgette**, washed and chopped into 2cm pieces

Drizzle of **balsamic vinegar**

**Rocket leaves** and **Parmesan cheese**, to serve (optional)

**Salt** and **pepper**

- **Preheat** the oven to 190°C (gas mark 5).

- **Drizzle** a roasting tray with the oil and put it in the oven for 10 minutes to heat up. Remove the tray and add the sweet potatoes. Return the tray to the oven and bake for 12 minutes.

- **Remove** the tray from the oven and scatter over the onion and red pepper. Return to the oven to cook for a further 12 minutes.

- **Meanwhile**, take each sausage in turn and push the meat out from inside the skin. Form the meat into little meatballs, you should have about three balls per sausage.

- **Remove** the tray from the oven and add the sausage meatballs. Sprinkle with the rosemary leaves before sliding the tray back in the oven for a further 12 minutes.

- **Remove** the tray from the oven, add the chopped courgette and return to the oven to cook for a final 5 minutes.

- **Remove** the tray from the oven, season and pile up a good mixture of roasted ingredients on your plates. Drizzle with a little balsamic vinegar, top with rocket and finish with swathes of Parmesan (if using). Sit back and marvel at your multi-coloured one-pot wonder.

# THE ULTIMATE BEEF STEW

We don't like to brag about our food, but, in this case, let us just say that this is the beef stew to bring all other beef stews to their knees. It's a classic recipe with a couple of little twists, such as the addition of star anise and orange peel, just to mix things up a bit.

## SERVES 6

6 tbsp **plain flour**

1.5 kg **beef cheek**, left whole (or braising beef)

4 tbsp **oil**

1 **onion**, peeled and finely chopped

2 **carrots**, peeled and finely chopped

2 **celery** sticks, finely chopped

2 dried **bay leaves**

2 fresh **thyme** sprigs

2 **star anise**

3cm piece of **orange peel**

6 large **tomatoes**, roughly chopped

1.25 litres **beef stock**

**Mashed Potato** (see page 19), to serve

**Green beans**, to serve

**Salt** and **pepper**

**Tip** the flour onto a plate and season well with salt and pepper. Behold the most majestic of all beef cuts (fanfare) ... Dust the beef cheeks in the seasoned flour so that they are well coated.

**Pour** half the oil into a large saucepan or casserole dish and heat over a medium to high heat. Once hot, add the beef cheeks (this may have to be done in batches) and fry on each side for about 3 minutes to brown all over. Remove the browned meat to a plate.

**Pour** the remaining oil into your casserole and add the onion, carrots and celery. Cook, stirring regularly, for 6–7 minutes until the onion is translucent and has softened. Add the bay leaves, thyme sprigs, star anise and orange peel. Continue to fry, stirring, for 2 minutes, before adding the chopped tomatoes and the browned meat.

**Pour** in the stock and bring to the boil. As the stew comes to the boil, spoon off any of the scum you see rising to the top (it's the stuff that looks like sea foam). Reduce the heat to low, place a lid on top and simmer for 2½ hours.

**Test** the meat to see if it is cooked enough: remove a piece of beef and pull a little away with a fork – it should almost fall apart. If it doesn't, then place the beef back in the casserole and continue simmering until it does. It shouldn't be much longer.

**Once** you are happy with the meat, use a slotted spoon to transfer the cooked pieces to a plate. Cling film the meat tightly.

**Place** a sieve over a large bowl or jug and tip the liquid from the pan through it. Using a ladle or a wooden spoon, squeeze the life out of the contents of the sieve before discarding. (This may seem a waste, and to a certain extent it is. If you prefer you can reserve the vegetables and add them back into the stew later.)

- **Pour** the strained liquid back into the saucepan and bring to the boil. Simmer the liquid until it has reduced by just over half. It should now be thick and glossy and the flavours should have intensified beautifully.

- **Remove** the cling film from the resting meat. Using two forks, pull apart the meat into large chunks and then tip it back into the reduced sauce. Coat the meat in the deliciously thick and dark gravy.

- **Serve** this dish, along with mashed potatoes and freshly cooked green beans, to only your very best friends or family – they are the only ones who deserve it.

- **Tip:** *Don't be put off by the cut of meat (cheek) used in this recipe. It transforms into the tenderest stewed meat you will ever have. All butchers will sell this cut, and there are now several supermarkets stocking it. If you must cook this dish with standard stewing meat, it will still taste great, just watch the cooking time as sometimes supermarket stewing meat can dry out early.*

# MAMMA MIA'S LASAGNE

The dish that other comfort foods eat when they need comfort. There is nobody on this planet who can resist the allure of a lasagne; hearty mince sandwiched between layers of soft pasta, all topped off with a luxurious, Parmesan-heavy cheese sauce. There is no question that to make a lasagne is a bit of a mission, but if you make this dish for your friends, you technically own them for a week and can set them menial tasks. That's how the Mafia started, apparently.

## SERVES 4

1 portion of **Multi-purpose Mince** (see page 38)

1 portion of **cheese sauce** (see page 30)

About 12 **lasagne sheets** (roughly 200g)

Generous grating of **Parmesan cheese**

**Preheat** the oven to 190°C (gas mark 5).

**For** this recipe you need to have quite a thick version of the mince recipe. Therefore it may be necessary to put the portion of Multi-purpose Mince in a saucepan, bring to the boil and simmer for about 20–30 minutes until most of the liquid has evaporated. You are looking to achieve a thick Bolognese with very little liquid.

**Spoon** one large spoonful of the cheese sauce into the base of your baking dish. Don't use too much – all you need is a very thin covering. Place your first layer of pasta on top. Try to be as neat as possible, but don't be afraid to overlap a little, or to break some of the pieces to fit. Spoon a third of your thickened mince on top of the uncooked pasta and spread to cover evenly.

**Top** the mince with another layer of pasta sheets before spooning on another third of your mince and spreading. Top again with more pasta before pouring over the remainder of your mince and topping once more with the last of your pasta sheets.

**Pour** your luxurious cheese sauce over the top of the final layer of pasta sheets. Scrape every last drop from your pan. Spread the cheese sauce evenly over the pasta and top with some grated Parmesan cheese before placing the dish in the oven.

**Bake** the lasagne in the preheated oven for 25–35 minutes until the top is golden. Remove from the oven and let the lasagne sit for at least 5 minutes before serving. This resting time allows everything to relax a little, which means that when it comes to dishing up you will be able to serve out satisfying squares instead of portions that fall to pieces.

# DIY TAKEAWAYS

You can't argue with takeaways. They're meals you can take away – to your home, or a street corner – and you don't have to make them. Delivery is even more magical, as they'll come to your couch.

They are not without their downsides, though. Takeaways can drain valuable money from your account, and they're also not that good for you. Our versions, although not health food, are definitely better for you – both for your wallet and your tummy, because you're in control of the ingredients that go in.

So next time you organise a night in, have a flick through this chapter, pool your money and cook up a home-made version of one of your favourite takeaways.

# PIRI-PIRI CHICKEN

Everyone likes a bit of Nando's chicken once in a while. Portugal, South Africa, Yorkshire: who really cares where piri-piri chicken actually originated from? All we know is that we love the sharp mixture of fire and vinegar on succulent flame-grilled chicken.

## SERVES 2

12 **red chillies**, stalks removed from all and seeds removed from 8 chillies

8 **garlic** cloves, peeled and left whole

1 **red onion**, peeled and roughly sliced

10 tbsp **oil**

2 tsp **sugar**

3 tbsp **red wine vinegar**

4 **chicken leg** joints, slashed a couple of times with a sharp knife

**Preheat** the oven to 200°C (gas mark 6).

**Put** the chillies, garlic and onion on a roasting tray and drizzle with 2 tablespoons of the oil. Roast in the oven for 15 minutes. Remove from the oven and leave to cool enough so that they can be handled.

**Chop up** all the roasted ingredients as fine as possible (or use a food processor). Then stir together with the remaining oil, sugar and red wine vinegar to get a roughly smooth liquid. Pour this marinade over the chicken and gently massage the meat with the prickly liquid until it is all well coated. Try to leave the chicken to marinate for at least 1 hour, but preferably leave it overnight.

**When** ready to cook, heat a griddle pan over a high heat until it begins to smoke (if you don't have a griddle pan, then cook under a grill set on high). Add the chicken pieces, in batches if necessary, and cook for 3–4 minutes on each side. You are looking for scorch marks on the chicken.

**Once** the chicken pieces have attained the 'Nando's' look, transfer them to a baking tray and place in the oven for 15 minutes until they are fully cooked through.

**Serve** your lip-smacking, sweat-inducing piri-piri chicken alongside Griddled Corn on the Cob (see page 154) and cooked rice while ceremoniously tearing up your Nando's loyalty card.

**Tip:** *The amount of chilli seeds you leave in the chillies when making the marinade will dictate how hot your sauce will be.*

# GRIDDLED CORN ON THE COB

Some say there is no practical reason to eat corn, as the body is unable to digest the kernel properly, and thus it passes through our bodies on a totally pointless journey. They are the same logicians who do suduko for fun and study applied mathematics. Corn on the cob has that deliciously sweet flavour, with each kernel popping in the mouth like an edible ray of sunshine (pictured on page 153).

**SERVES 4**

2 whole **corn on the cobs**, husks removed and cut in half

2 tbsp **oil**

**Bring** a large saucepan of water to boiling point. Drop in the cob halves and boil for 4 minutes. Remove and pat dry.

**Heat** a griddle pan over a high heat until it is smoking. Rub the cob pieces with the oil and cook on the hot griddle for 5 minutes, turning a couple of times, until they are lightly scorched all over.

**Serve** alongside the Piri-Piri Chicken and there you have it, takeaway heaven.

**Tip:** *If you don't have a griddle pan, then cook the corn under a grill set to maximum and grill for 5 minutes, turning a couple of times, until they are lightly scorched.*

# NO.42 ALL-PURPOSE EGG-FRIED RICE

Here's a recipe that's so versatile you might end up trying to get it to fix your door, do your dissertation and talk to people you fancy in clubs. It won't do any of that, but when it comes to using up leftovers lurking at the bottom of the fridge, it can't be beaten. Be it cold sausages or shrivelled-up vegetables, soy-sauce-enhanced fried rice is the perfect vehicle for delicious disposal.

## SERVES 2

2 **eggs**

3 tbsp light **soy sauce**

5 tsp **sesame oil**

3 tbsp **vegetable oil**

3 **spring onions**

2 **garlic** cloves, peeled and finely chopped

400g leftover cooked **rice**

*Tip: You can add anything from leftover roast chicken to sweetcorn to this recipe. Just remember that anything raw goes in before the rice, and anything cooked can be thrown in afterwards because it only has to be warmed through.*

**Crack** the eggs into a bowl. Add 1 tablespoon of the soy sauce and 2 teaspoons of the sesame oil. Beat together with a fork until well combined.

**Heat** 1 tablespoon of the oil in your largest frying pan over a high heat. Once smoking, add the egg and let it bubble up and set as it hits the heat. Let it cook on one side for 2 minutes and then break up the egg and stir it around. You are aiming for a kind of scrambled omelette. This should take only 1–2 minutes more. Immediately remove to a clean plate.

**Take** your spring onions and trim off the stringy bits at the ends. You are going to use both the green and white part of the onion, but at different stages in the recipe, so slice all your spring onions into thin disks, but keep the white and the green separate.

**Place** your frying pan back over a high heat and pour in the remaining vegetable oil. Once hot, add the whites of the spring onions and the garlic. Leave to cook and sizzle for a minute, just long enough to colour the garlic a little. Add the cooked rice and fry, stirring like a maniac, for 3 minutes. You are aiming for all of the grains to become separated. Use your spoon to break down any clumps that may have occurred.

**Turn** off the heat, add the cooked eggs, green parts of the spring onions and the remaining soy sauce and sesame oil.

**This** is a meal in its own right but you could always serve it with the Sticky Honeyed Chicken (see page 157) or a stir-fry of your choice.

# STICKY HONEYED CHICKEN

This dish is as rich and sumptuous as they come. The moist chicken is virtually lacquered by the sticky and savoury sauce.

**SERVES 4**

3 tbsp **oil**

4 **chicken thighs**, skin on and bone in

4 **chicken legs**, skin on and bone in

4 **spring onions**, white parts only, roughly chopped

2 **garlic** cloves, peeled and finely chopped

1 tbsp **honey**

5 tbsp light **soy sauce** (about 75ml)

1 **red chilli**, deseeded and finely sliced, to garnish (optional)

**Heat** half the oil in a large frying pan over a medium to high heat. Once hot, add the chicken pieces and cook for about 5 minutes until brown all over. (Do this in batches so that you don't overcrowd the meat.) Once browned, remove the chicken pieces to a plate.

**Wipe** the pan with a little kitchen paper, then pour in the remaining oil and heat over a medium to high heat again. Once hot, add the chopped spring onions and the garlic. Fry, stirring regularly, for 1 minute. Tip the chicken back into the pan and stir to coat with the garlic and spring onions.

**Pour** in 5 tablespoons of water, the honey and soy sauce. Bring to the boil and cover the pan. If you don't have a lid big enough then cover with a bit of foil. Leave to cook for about 10–12 minutes. Remove the lid (or foil) – the sauce should have reduced a little and started to coat the chicken. Continue cooking for a further 3–4 minutes uncovered so that the sauce reduces and the meat is nicely coated. Do not leave the dish at this point as the honey may burn.

**Serve** up your chicken pieces sprinkled with the sliced red chilli (if using), along with some napkins or kitchen paper, because there is no other way to eat this other than with your fingers. If you are feeling greedy, serve this with the No. 42 all-purpose egg-fried rice on page 155.

# CHICKEN AND SWEET POTATO CURRY £££

Curries don't just belong to the Indian sub-continent, and this recipe proves it. This is more of a Pacific Rim-style recipe. Even though some of the ingredients might sound a tad exotic, rest assured all of them can be found in most major supermarkets.

## SERVES 4

4 **chicken thighs**, skinless,chopped into bite-size pieces

2 tbsp mild **curry powder**

2–3 tbsp **oil**

1 **red onion**, peeled and finely chopped

4 **garlic** cloves, peeled and finely chopped

Thumb-size piece of fresh **ginger**, peeled and grated

2 **lemongrass** stalks, trimmed and finely chopped

1 **red chilli**, split down the middle

1 x 400ml tin of **coconut milk**

2 **sweet potatoes**, peeled and chopped into large chunks

1 tbsp **fish sauce**

Juice of 1 **lime**

250g baby **spinach**

**Jasmine rice**, to serve

**Salt** and **pepper**

**Put** the chicken thighs in a dish and sprinkle over the curry powder. Mix the pieces around so that they are evenly coated with the powder. Leave the chicken to infuse while you get on with the rest of the dish.

**Heat** 2 tablespoons of the oil in a large saucepan over a medium to high heat. Once hot, add the red onion and fry, stirring regularly, for 3 minutes. Add the garlic, ginger, lemongrass and split chilli. Continue stirring and frying for another 3 minutes. All the vegetables should begin to soften.

**Increase** the heat to maximum and add the chicken pieces. Fry over a high heat for about 2 minutes, turning regularly. Add the remaining oil at this point if you think it is needed. Once the chicken has taken on a little colour, season generously with salt and pepper and pour in the coconut milk. Half fill the empty can with water and pour that in too. Bring the curry to the boil before reducing the heat to a simmer.

**Add** the sweet potato and simmer the curry for 10–15 minutes until the chicken is cooked through and the sweet potato pieces are cooked. Add the fish sauce and the lime juice, then taste and adjust the seasoning if needed. Take the pan off the heat and stir in the baby spinach until wilted.

**Serve** your colourful and tasty curry on top of bowls of cooked jasmine rice.

# SOY-GLAZED PORK

This recipe works for the barbecue just as well as it does for the grill. The marinade also works incredibly well for all cuts of pork, from loin to chop.

**SERVES 4**

6 tbsp light **soy sauce**

2 tbsp **honey**

2 tsp **sesame oil**

Small thumb-size piece of **fresh ginger**, peeled and grated

3 **garlic** cloves, peeled and finely chopped

800g **pork belly**, cut into 2cm strips

4 **spring onions**, white part only, roughly chopped, to garnish (optional)

2 **red chillies**, deseeded and finely chopped, to garnish (optional)

Cooked **rice** and boiled **broccoli**, to serve

**Pour** the soy sauce, honey and sesame oil into a dish. Add the ginger and garlic and mix well with a spoon until the honey has dissolved into the soy sauce. Add the slices of pork belly and leave to marinate for at least 1 hour, but preferably overnight.

**When** ready to cook, preheat the grill to its highest setting. Place a sheet of foil on the grill tray and lay the pork slices on top of it. If some of the marinade is left behind, don't worry, it will be used later. Place the pork under the grill and cook for 7–8 minutes until golden and lightly charred. Remove the tray and turn the pork slices. Spoon over any remaining marinade left in the bowl at this point before returning the pork under the grill and cooking for a further 7–8 minutes. The pork should be glistening and caramelised.

**Remove** the pork from the grill, garnish with the chopped spring onions and chopped red chillies (if using) and serve up with freshly cooked rice and boiled broccoli. Yumma, yumma.

# TERIYAKI SALMON

This must be one of the most popular dishes in the world, and it's easy to see why; it's quick, delicious and easy to cook. Even if you are terrified of cooking fish or sampling new flavours, we suggest you cook this dish as it will only serve to encourage your gastro-journey.

## SERVES 2

4 tbsp light **soy sauce**

2 tsp **honey**

2 **garlic** cloves, peeled and finely chopped

1 tbsp **rice wine vinegar** (cider or white vinegar will work as well)

2 tsp **sesame oil**

2 skinless **salmon fillets**, weighing about 200g each

Cooked **rice**, to serve

**Pour** the soy sauce and honey into a bowl and add the garlic, vinegar and sesame oil. Use a spoon to mix the ingredients until the honey has dissolved into the soy sauce. Place your salmon fillets in the mixture and leave to sit for at least 15 minutes or a maximum of 1 hour.

**When** ready to cook, preheat the grill to maximum. Line a grill try with tin foil. Place the salmon fillets on top, leaving behind a lot of the marinade. Place the fish under the hot grill and cook for 5 minutes.

**Carefully** turn the fish before spooning on as much of the remaining marinade left in the bowl as possible. Place back under the grill and cook for a further 5 minutes.

**Remove** the fish from the grill and leave to stand for 2 minutes before sliding the fish off the foil and onto a pile of steaming rice. Serve with a bit of the 'Pickled' Cucumber Salad (pictured on the opposite page) and feel your culinary qi growing stronger.

# A KIND OF 'PICKLED' CUCUMBER SALAD

This is a deliciously balanced salad that is the perfect foil to any dish that you feel is very heavy. Any dish that involves roasting or browning will be perfectly set off with this accompaniment.

## SERVES 2

5 tbsp **white wine vinegar**

1 tsp **sugar**

2 tsp **salt**

1 **cucumber**

**Mix** all the ingredient, apart from the cucumber, in a bowl thoroughly so that the sugar and the salt dissolve.

**Chop** off both ends of the cucumber. Either holding the cucumber in your hand, or laying it on your chopping board, run your peeler the full length of the cucumber to produce a long, thin strip. Repeat the process on the same side until you come to the seeds. At this point roll the cucumber 90 degrees and repeat the process. Continue peeling until you are left with the seeded core of the cucumber and a pile of thin, ribbon-like cucumber strips.

**Place** the cucmber strips in a bowl and pour the vinegar mixture over the top. Leave the cucumber to sit in the mixture, turning a couple of times, for at least 10 minutes. Serve with the Teriyaki Salmon (see opposite) alongside freshly steamed rice.

# LAMB KEBABS

Let's not beat around the bush here. Kebabs are the foodstuff of drunks and, err, students. That gently rotating, mysterious-meat beacon has swayed us all towards it at one time or another. However, here we have a recipe that shows kebabs are not just the fodder of drunks; they can actually be a very high-class dish that can be enjoyed sober too. True story.

## SERVES 4

1 tbsp ground **cumin**

3 tbsp **oil**

3 **garlic** cloves, peeled and finely chopped

1 kg **lamb leg**, chopped into large chunks

1 **red onion**, peeled and roughly sliced into large chunks

**Salt** and **pepper**

## TO SERVE

**Pitta bread**

200g ready-made **garlic and onion dip**

**Iceberg lettuce**, shredded

**Chilli sauce** (optional)

**Put** the cumin, oil and garlic in a bowl with a generous amount of salt and pepper. Add the chunks of lamb and the red onion. Mix well to coat all of the pieces. Leave the meat to marinate for at least 1 hour, but preferably overnight.

**Preheat** your grill to its maximum setting.

**Line** your grill tray with foil and tip the marinated meat onto it. Place under the hot grill and cook for 8–9 minutes. The meat should begin to colour. Turn the meat and continue to grill for a further 5 minutes.

**Toast** your pitta breads and cut them open. Spoon some garlic and onion dip into the bottom and spread it roughly around the sides. Add pieces of meat along with some chilli sauce (if using), shredded lettuce and another drizzle of the garlic and onion dip.

**Neck** 6 pints of lager and tuck in.

# INDIAN LAMB CURRY

Contrary to popular belief, you do not need an entire continent's worth of spices to prepare a curry. Just stick with this recipe and smile knowingly when all your friends marvel at your internationally influenced palate. With slow cooking, the best meat to buy is often the cheaper and fattier cuts. Try using diced shoulder or neck of lamb for this recipe.

## SERVES 4

6 tbsp **oil**

2 **onions**, peeled and grated

5 **garlic** cloves, peeled and very finely chopped

Large thumb-size piece of fresh **ginger**, peeled and very finely chopped

2 **green chillies**, split lengthways, but still held together at the top

1½ tbsp **garam masala**

1 tbsp **ground cumin**

1 tbsp **ground turmeric**

800g diced **lamb** (neck or shoulder work best)

4 **tomatoes**, roughly chopped

Large handful of fresh **coriander**, chopped

Cooked **basmati rice**, to serve

**Salt**

**Heat** the oil in a large saucepan or casserole dish over a medium heat. Once hot, add the onions and a generous pinch of salt. Cook the onions, stirring regularly, for 12–15 minutes until they become lightly coloured and incredibly soft.

**Add** the garlic, ginger and green chillies. Fry for a further 4 minutes, stirring regularly, before spooning in the spices. It is very important to 'cook out' the spices for 1 minute, so fry, constantly stirring to avoid burning. Increase the heat to maximum, then add the diced lamb. Stir well to combine for 1 minute, then add the tomatoes.

**Reduce** the heat a little and add half a glass of water to the saucepan. Bring the liquid up to the boil, then reduce to a simmer. Place a lid on top and leave to cook for a minimum of 1 hour. (It can go on cooking for double that time if you keep adding a little water every now and then to prevent it from drying out.) The longer the curry is cooked, the better it becomes.

**Add** the chopped coriander just before serving with cooked basmati rice . . . and then delete the curry takeaway number from your telephone.

**Tip:** *More often than not, curries taste better the day after they have been cooked because the flavours settle and intensify. So if you can cook this the night before, leave it to cool completely before refrigerating. When ready to eat, just tip the curry back into the saucepan and bring to the boil over a medium heat. Simmer for 2–3 minutes and enjoy your fully matured curry.*

# GOOD OLD BURGER 'N' SAUCE

It is no secret that Big Macs are delicious, but it is less well known that the undeniable flavour comes not from the meat patties, nor the buns, but mostly from the secret sauce. That's why we've included our version of the tasty condiment. These burgers cook just as well on the barbecue as they do in the pan. Take them, and the sauce, along to any summer get-together and you will soon be heralded as the new Burger King (apologies, we couldn't resist).

## MAKES 4 BURGERS

1 kg **minced beef**

1 **red onion**, peeled and grated

2 tbsp **oil**

4 burger **baps**

2 tbsp shop-bought **tomato relish**

4 tbsp **mayonnaise**

1 **shallot**, peeled and finely diced

1 tbsp **white wine vinegar**

**Salt** and **pepper**

## TO SERVE

1 **tomato**, thinly sliced

1 jar of **gherkins**

1 round **lettuce**, leaves separated or shredded

**Put** the minced beef, onion and generous amounts of salt and pepper into a large bowl. Mix well with your hands for at least 2 minutes – this mixing will help keep the burgers together.

**Divide** the mixture into 4 equal balls. Shape each ball into a patty roughly 12cm across and 3cm thick.

**Heat** the oil in a large non-stick frying pan over a medium to high heat. Once hot, add your burgers. If your pan is not big enough to accommodate all of the burgers at once then you will have to cook them in batches.

**Fry** your burgers for 5 minutes on both sides. Reduce the heat to medium and continue to cook for a further 4 minutes on each side. Remove the burgers to a plate and leave to rest while you continue with the remaining components.

**Slice** the burger baps in half and place them, cut side down, into the same pan that the burgers were cooked in. Fry over a medium heat for 2 minutes. This may well have to be done in batches. Once the buns are done, place them to one side.

**In** a small bowl, mix together the tomato relish, mayonnaise, diced shallot and white wine vinegar. This is how easy it is to create your favourite burger sauce!

**Now** you have all the components in front of you to build your ultimate burger, including our classic serving suggestions, go forth and make the best darned burger you can.

# TOMATO, MOZZARELLA AND BASIL PIZZA

Creating a pizza with a thin, crispy base generally involves stoking an oven to the temperature of the earth's core or purchasing a pizza stone. Alas, we have done away with these 'barriers to entry'. All you need to cook our pizza is a non-stick frying pan and an oven.

**MAKES 4**

1 x 7g sachet of dried **yeast**

1 tsp **sugar**

400g **strong white flour**, plus a little extra for dusting

2 tsp **salt**

**Olive oil**, for frying

2 portions of **Simple Tomato Sauce** (see page 29)

3 balls of **mozzarella**

Dried **oregano**, for sprinkling

Fresh **basil leaves**, to serve (optional)

**Measure** out 300ml of warm water. You want the water to be lukewarm so that it doesn't kill the yeast.

**Empty** the sachet of yeast into a bowl and pour over about a quarter of the warm water. Mix well with a whisk or fork before pouring in the remaining water and the sugar. Stir the mixture so that all of the components are well mixed.

**Place** the flour and salt in a bowl and pour in the yeast mixture. Combine well with a wooden spoon before rolling up your sleeves and kneading with your hands. As the dough comes together, tip it out onto a lightly floured surface so you can really get some leverage. Knead for about 5 minutes before bringing the dough together in a ball and placing in a clean bowl. Cover the bowl with a clean tea towel or cling film and place somewhere warm for a couple of hours.

**After** 2 hours the dough should have doubled in size. Remove the cover and tip the dough out onto a lightly floured surface. Knead the dough again for 30 seconds just to knock out the air. Separate the dough into 4 balls.

**Preheat** the oven to 190°C (gas mark 5).

**Using** either your fingers, a rolling pin or an extravagant tossing-in-the-air technique, form a circle about 1 ½ cm thick and about 25cm in diameter (it must fit into your frying pan).

**Heat** a good glug of oil in your frying pan over a medium to high heat. Once hot, carefully place your dough in the pan. At this point you can use a spoon to push the dough out towards the edges of the pan. Fry the dough like this for 2–3 minutes, just long enough for it to take on a golden and crispy appearance. Flip your dough over and fry for a further 2–3 minutes on the other side before sliding out your crisp pizza base onto a baking tray.

**You** can choose now whether you want to fry off all of your bases at once (also see Tip), and have a mass bake-off later, or top the one you have just done, and put it in the oven while you fry the other bases. The decision is yours and may well depend on your levels of patience.

**Whatever** you choose to do, when you're ready to bake you need to top the base with a generous amount of tomato sauce, chunks of ripped mozzarella and a scattering of dried oregano. Place the pizza in the oven and bake for about 10 minutes until the mozzarella has melted and is bubbling.

**Remove** your pizza from the oven and scatter with fresh basil (if using), slice and scoff.

**Tip:** *Once the pizza bases have been fried, they can be cooled and frozen if you don't want to use them all in one sitting.*

**Variations:** *There really is no wrong you can do in terms of toppings for pizza. Try the usual toppings, such as salami, olives, anchovies and basil, but don't be afraid to experiment – one of our team remembers their university pizzeria selling the rather unique chip and mozzarella pizza.*

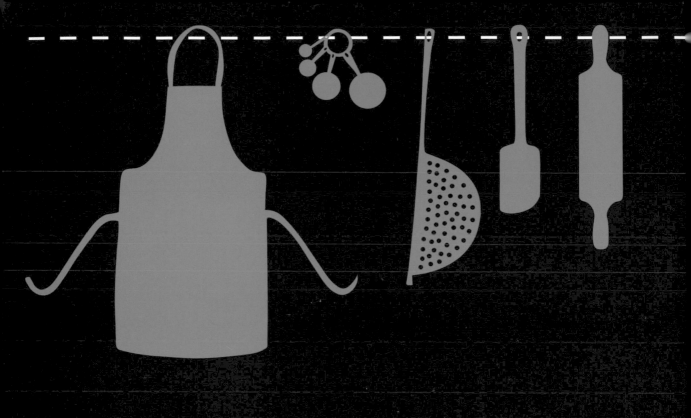

# SWEET STUFF

Desserts and sweet treats are so often seen as luxuries rather than necessities. Well, boo hoo to that. There is nothing better than spending a couple of productive hours at the weekend whipping together a delicious cake or mousse with which to indulge yourself and your friends.

The best thing about most desserts is that, once you've made them, they keep for several days, so when you have a craving for something sweet you can just reach into the fridge or Tupperware for the leftovers of your toil.

There is also much to be said for the process of making desserts. Many people find the whole experience very calming and satisfying. So, when looking for the perfect excuse to stop working on your dissertation, look no further than this chapter for a stress-busting and delicious way to dodge boring work.

# ALL-AMERICAN PANCAKES

These are the thicker pancakes that Americans seem intent on serving each other in towering stacks smothered with maple syrup and topped with crispy bacon. We suggest a more restrained stack, served on a hungover Sunday morning, doused in maple syrup with a dollop of yoghurt and a scattering of blueberries. It will remind you why it's good to be human and pull you through your hangover.

**MAKES 8**

150g **plain flour**

1 tsp **baking powder**

2 tbsp **caster sugar**

1 **egg**

150ml **milk**

40g **butter**, melted

**Oil**, for frying

**TO SERVE** (any of the below go very well)

**Blueberries**

**Maple syrup**

**Pecans**

**Bananas**

**Natural yoghurt**

**Clotted cream**

Cooked **bacon** – if you've lost all sense of reality

**Tip** the flour into a bowl and add the baking powder and caster sugar. Mix to combine.

**In** a separate bowl, crack the egg into the milk and whisk with a fork until they are well mixed.

**Pour** half of the milk and egg into the flour and combine well with a wooden spoon. Pour in the remaining milk mix and continue to beat well with a wooden spoon to form a thick batter. Add the melted butter and stir to combine. You should now have a batter with the consistency of a thick smoothie.

**Heat** a very small amount of oil in the bottom of your best non-stick frying pan over a medium to high heat. Once hot, begin adding small amounts of batter with a ladle (or a big spoon). If you pour consistently in one spot then a small, even circle should appear – you are aiming for a 5mm-thick pancake.

**Leave** the pancake to fry on one side for about 3 minutes. You should begin to see little air bubbles come to the surface. Flip and cook for a further 3 minutes on the other side. Remove the pancake to a plate and keep warm while you cook the remaining pancakes. Once you become more practised at this, you will be able to cook 2 or 3 at the same time.

**Serve** piles of pancakes stacked high, smothered in whatever topping you desire, and feel the will to live slowly return.

# NANA'S SCONES

When crazed university shenanigans are all getting a bit much, it's time for afternoon tea and scones just the way Nana used to make them. Once you have baked these scones you will realise how incredibly easy they are.

**MAKES 20**

500g **plain flour**, plus a little extra for dusting

75g cold **butter**, cut into cubes

75g **caster sugar**

5 tsp **baking powder**

3 **eggs**

250ml **milk**

**Strawberry jam** or **golden syrup** and **clotted** or **whipped cream**, to serve

**Preheat** the oven to 220°C (gas mark 7).

**Put** the flour in a bowl and add the butter. Using your fingers and thumbs, work the butter into the flour until your mixture resembles fine breadcrumbs. This may take a little bit of time. Once you have the correct consistency, stir in the caster sugar and baking powder.

**Beat** 2 of the eggs in a separate bowl. Pour the beaten eggs and the milk into the mixture and stir with a wooden spoon to form a dough. Lightly flour a clean surface and tip the dough out onto it. Knead the dough for 20 seconds just to make sure all of the ingredients are well incorporated.

**Either** using the palms of your hands or a rolling pin, roll or push the dough out to a thickness of about 3cm. Use a cutter or glass to cut out scones about 8cm wide, and place them on a baking tray. To maximise your dough, rework it once you have cut as many scones out as possible.

**Beat** the remaining egg in a small bowl. Once you have all your scones lined up on a baking tray, brush the tops lightly with the beaten egg. Bake in the preheated oven for 15 minutes until the scones have risen and are beautifully golden on top.

**Serve** warm with lashings of heart-attack-inducing condiments.

**Variations:** *The sky is the limit when it comes to sweet variations; just add dried fruit or fresh berries. As for savoury scones, just leave out the caster sugar and add a pinch of salt, grated cheese and some fried bacon pieces instead.*

# RASPBERRY AND WHITE CHOCOLATE MUFFINS

Muffins can be either savoury or sweet. Having said that, what could be better than a sweet muffin studded with white chocolate and raspberries? In fact, be careful – if you make this recipe, you may never eat savoury food again.

## MAKES 8–12

110g **raspberries**

125g **caster sugar**, plus 1 tbsp

250g **self-raising flour**

2 tsp **baking powder**

50g cold **butter**, cut into cubes

1 **egg**

175ml **milk**

100g **white chocolate**, broken into small pieces

Small handful of chopped **pistachios** (optional)

**Preheat** the oven to 180°C (gas mark 4).

**Put** the raspberries in a bowl and sprinkle with the tablespoon of sugar. Using the back of a fork, roughly mash the raspberries and sugar together. Don't go overboard and create a purée; there should still be some lumps of raspberry in there. Leave to one side.

**Put** the remaining sugar, flour and baking powder in a large bowl and stir to combine. Add the butter, and using your fingers and thumbs, rub it into the flour mixture until it resembles fine breadcrumbs – this may take a few minutes.

**In** a bowl, crack the egg into the milk and use a fork to beat together well. Pour the liquid into the dry mixture and, using a wooden spoon, gently bring it all together until just combined. Avoid overmixing, otherwise you will end up with a very dense muffin. Add the chocolate pieces and the crushed raspberries and fold briefly to combine.

**Dollop** the mixture equally into a muffin tin lined with paper cases. Sprinkle chopped pistachios on top (if using) and bake in the preheated oven for 20 minutes or until the muffins are beautifully risen, golden on top and a knife inserted into the middle of a muffin comes out clean.

**Serve** warm, cold, chilled, blistering – doesn't matter, they are delicious any which way.

**Tip:** *These muffins can be a grab-and-go breakfast or a perfect sugar injection halfway through double lectures.*

# THE ULTIMATE VANILLA CUPCAKES

Cupcakes are essentially small cakes with an uneven ratio of sponge to icing; and that's what makes them so delicious. Designing and decorating them is what makes them so fun.

**MAKES 12**

100g **butter**, softened at room temperature

100g **caster sugar**

2 **eggs**

120g **self-raising flour**

2 tbsp **milk**

2 tsp **vanilla extract**

**FOR THE BUTTERCREAM**

150g **butter**, softened at room temperature

2 tsp **liquid glucose**

250g **icing sugar**

2 tsp **vanilla extract**

Few drops of **food colouring**

Assorted **decorations** (silver pearls, crystallised rose petals, sprinkles)

**Preheat** the oven to 180°C (gas mark 4).

**Tip** the butter into a bowl and add the sugar. Use a hand whisk or a wooden spoon to cream the ingredients together until pale white and creamy. This should only take 2–3 minutes of elbow grease if your butter is at room temperature.

**Crack** in 1 of the eggs and whisk in thoroughly before adding the second. The mixture may curdle a bit at this point; don't worry, it will work itself out. Tip in the flour and use a wooden spoon to work it into the sugar mix. Add the milk and the vanilla extract and continue beating until you have a smooth batter.

**Divide** the mixture equally between 12 cupcake moulds lined with paper cases. Bake in the preheated oven for 12 minutes or until the tops are golden brown and a knife inserted into the middle of a cupcake comes out clean. Leave the cupcakes to cool to room temperature.

**Meanwhile**, make the buttercream. Put all the ingredients, except the food colouring, in a bowl and slowly bring them together using a wooden spoon. As the icing sugar is worked into the butter you can speed up your mixing motion until you are finally beating the icing together.

**Add** the food colouring drop by drop, as some are more potent than others. Experiment with different colours but make sure you beat the colouring in thoroughly before spooning the icing into a piping bag fitted with a star-shaped nozzle (or simply snip off a tiny corner from a plastic sandwich bag). Leave to one side until needed.

**Once** the cupcakes have cooled to room temperature, let your artistic side take over and decorate your cupcakes with the icing and whatever sprinkles you like.

**Variation:** *For decorations, sprinkles, pearls and petals are fun, but Maltesers could be even better. Other combinations that work are maple syrup and walnuts, pecan and banana, strawberry and grated dark chocolate or salted peanuts. Hell, why not add a sparkler to celebrate Guy Fawkes Night!*

# PEANUT BUTTER AND CHOCOLATE COOKIES

Peanut butter and chocolate . . . What's not to like? This recipe results in cookies that have a crispy edge and a gooey centre. If you don't like this type of cookie then you can just cook them for a little bit longer, but we think you'd be mad to do so.

**MAKES 12**

Generous splash
of **milk**

125g light **soft brown
sugar**

125g **butter**

100g smooth **peanut
butter**

1 tsp **salt**

250g **plain flour**

1 tsp **bicarbonate
of soda**

1 **egg**

150g **milk chocolate
chips**

**Preheat** the oven to 180°C (gas mark 4).

**Put** the milk, sugar, butter, peanut butter and salt in a large saucepan over a medium heat. As the butters and sugar begin to melt into the milk, stir to combine. Once all the ingredients are well incorporated, take the pan off the heat and allow to cool briefly.

**Place** the flour and bicarbonate of soda in a large bowl. Pour in the melted peanut butter mix and stir this into the flour. Crack the egg into the bowl and add the chocolate chips. Mix thoroughly until you end up with a dough-like consistency.

**Take** a golf-ball-size portion of the mixture and roll it in your palms to form a ball. Gently flatten the ball until it becomes a disk about 1cm thick. Place on a non-stick baking tray. Repeat the process with the remaining mixture, making sure you leave a couple of inches between each soon-to-be cookie.

**Bake** in the preheated oven for 15 minutes or until golden brown. Remove the cookies from the oven and place on a rack to cool for a few minutes before devouring.

# BANANA AND CHOCOLATE LOAF

You can't beat bananas — they're cheap, filling and very good at dealing with hangovers. The only problem is that they're a little time sensitive. Well, here's a recipe that will use up the bananas in the bowl that have gone so black you feel you need carbon dating to remind you of when you bought them.

**SERVES 6**

300g **self-raising flour**

150g cold **butter**, cut into cubes, plus extra for greasing

150g **caster sugar**

**3 eggs**

3 old, very **ripe bananas**, peeled

Splash of **milk**

100g **chocolate** of your choice, broken into pieces

- **Preheat** the oven to 190°C (gas mark 5).

- **Prepare** a 25cm x 10cm loaf tin by greasing it with a little butter.

- **Chute** (posh word for tip) the flour into a large bowl and add the butter. Using your fingers and thumbs, rub the butter into the flour until you are left with a mixture that resembles breadcrumbs. Don't worry overly if there are a few lumps here and there.

- **Add** the sugar, eggs and the mushy bananas and mix well with a wooden spoon or fork. You're aiming to mush the bananas into the flour mixture and to incorporate the sugar and eggs to form a smooth batter.

- **Pour** in the milk, just enough to loosen the whole mixture into an inviting batter before dropping in your chocolate pieces.

- **Pour** the mixture into the loaf tin and bake in the preheated oven for 35 minutes or until a knife inserted into the middle comes out clean. (Keep an eye on the loaf during the baking process – if it is still uncooked on the inside but is colouring too much on the outside then simply cover with foil.)

- **Remove** the loaf from the oven and leave to cool in the tin for at least 10 minutes. Serve with a cup of tea.

- **Tip:** *It really is no understatement to say you must use old bananas; fresh bananas simply won't work. As soon as your bananas are at least 50 per cent black, they're good to use for this recipe.*

# CHOCOLATE CRISPY CAKES

Just when you thought the days of Rice Krispie cakes were over, along come Student Beans to reinvent the classic by adding an extra chocolatey dimension.

**MAKES 12**

50g **butter**

300g **marshmallows**

½ x 550g packet of **Coco Pops**

75g **white chocolate**

75g **dark chocolate**

**Place** the butter and marshmallows in a saucepan over a medium heat. As the marshmallows warm up they will begin to melt into a sticky gloop. Encourage the melting with a few stirs using a wooden spoon. Once melted, remove from the heat.

**Pour** the Coco Pops into a large bowl, and immediately pour over the melted marshmallow mixture and mix well to coat. Tip the mixture into a baking tray lined with baking parchment and, using the back of a spoon, press down to create an even surface.

**Break** the white chocolate and the dark chocolate into separate bowls. Melt the chocolates in the microwave, one at a time, using short bursts of power. Using two separate spoons, drizzle the melted chocolates over the setting cake to create your very own Jackson Pollock tribute.

**Leave** the cake to set at room temperature for at least 2 hours, before removing from the tray, chopping into individual squares and amazing your friends with this retro dessert.

# ROCKY ROAD

This is one of those desserts that feels as if it should come in a children's party bag. But for all its juvenility, nobody can deny how deliciously satisfying a slice of this is.

## MAKES 20

250g good-quality **milk chocolate**

150g good-quality **dark chocolate** (about 70% cocoa solids)

75g **butter**

Small handful of **raisins**

1 x 250g packet of **digestives** (minus a couple to snack on!), broken up into small pieces

2 small handfuls of **pink and white mini marshmallows**

**Line** an ovenproof dish or deep baking tray with baking parchment.

**Place** a heatproof bowl over a saucepan of gently simmering water, making sure the base of the bowl does not touch the water. Add both chocolates and the butter to the bowl and leave the mixture to melt over the boiling water for about 8 minutes without stirring.

**When** the chocolate and butter have almost all melted, carefully remove the bowl from the top of the saucepan and mix the contents together with a spatula or wooden spoon until you are left with a smooth mixture. Transfer one-third of the mixture to a clean bowl and set aside.

**Add** the remaining ingredients to the main chocolate bowl, and fold them in as evenly as possible. Tip the mixture into your lined dish or tray and pat down with a spoon to level out the surface. Pour the reserved melted chocolate over the top and spread to cover as much as possible.

**Leave** the Rocky Road to cool to room temperature before removing from its tray and chopping into deliciously juvenile pieces.

**Variation:** *We have opted to add raisins, marshmallows and digestives to our Rocky Road, but feel free to let your imagination run wild – experiment with different textures and flavours. Dried fruits and nuts will never fail, but for the adventurous, why not add a honeycomb chocolate bar?*

# BLACK FOREST PINT-O-TRIFLE

This is about as random as we can get. Yet sometimes from the insane comes the sublime, and I think we may well have just pulled off a blinder here. Procure yourself some half-pint glasses from your local and make up your own mind.

## SERVES 6

10 sheets of **gelatine leaf**

750ml diluted **cherry cordial** or **fresh juice**

1 x ready-made plain **chocolate cake**

2 x 425g **tins of black cherries**, drained and rinsed under cold water

150ml **double cream**, lightly whipped

Grated **dark chocolate**, to garnish

**Immerse** the gelatine leaves in cold water for at least 5 minutes, by which time they should have softened considerably.

**In** a small saucepan, warm the cherry cordial over a medium heat, just to the point when you can see a little steam rising off it. You should be able to dip your finger quickly into the liquid without it being uncomfortable.

**Take** a quarter of the soaked gelatine leaves from the cold water and squeeze to remove any excess liquid. Whisk the gelatine into the cherry cordial to dissolve. Add the remaining gelatine and whisk throughly until all of it has dissolved into the liquid. Leave the mixture to cool to room temperature.

**Meanwhile**, cut out circles of chocolate cake that fit snugly into the base of the glasses. You may need to push the cake in with your fingers – this doesn't have to be an overly neat job. Aim for a layer of cake that takes up just less than a third of the glass (you may have to put one layer on top of another). Once all your glasses have a base layer, and your cherry juice has cooled to room temperature, you're ready to start construction.

**Pour** a little of the cherry liquid into each glass, just to moisten the cake. Drop a few cherries into each glass and pour enough liquid in to almost cover the cherries. Place the glasses in the fridge for 30 minutes to set this layer. Remove the glasses from the fridge and repeat this process twice more to create two more set layers. When adding the last layer, make sure you leave about 2cm clear at the top for the cream. Place the glasses back in the fridge for a further 30 minutes, before removing and topping with the softly whipped cream. The trifles can be served immediately or placed in the fridge overnight; just grate a little chocolate on top of them before serving.

# 'MUGGED' CHOCOLATE HAZELNUT MOUSSE

*'If you don't like Nutella, you're dead to me.'  Dalai Lama (apparently)*

Dressing up Nutella as a 'mature' mousse makes it seem OK to shovel spoonful after spoonful into our mouths — something we're all well practised at from childhood raids of that ubiquitous jar of Nutella.

## MAKES 6

250g **chocolate hazelnut spread** (we like Nutella)

A splash of **milk**

120ml **double cream**, plus extra for serving

2 **egg whites**

50g **caster sugar**

100g chopped **hazelnuts**, to serve

**Put** the Nutella and milk in a saucepan over a medium heat. As the mixture warms up, stir with a wooden spoon to combine into a smooth mixture. Remove from the heat, scrape the mixture into a bowl and leave it to cool a little.

**In** a separate clean bowl, whisk up the double cream so that when you lift the whisk it leaves soft peaks. Leave the whipped cream in the fridge until needed.

**Put** the egg whites in a clean bowl and whisk (either by hand or using an electric whisk) for a couple of minutes or until the whites have turned into a thick white foam. At this point, add a teaspoon of sugar and whisk again for 20 seconds before adding another 2 teaspoons of sugar and whisking again. The sugar should begin to thicken the whites. Add the remaining sugar gradually while whisking thoroughly, until you are left with a thick and glossy meringue mixture.

**Time** for everything to come together. The Nutella and milk mixture should have cooled a little but still be reasonably loose. Using a large metal spoon or spatula, mix in the whipped double cream until it is fully incorporated. If you find yourself in trouble with lots of lumps of cream, briefly use a whisk to break them up. Once the cream has been incorporated, dollop in one-third of the meringue mix and combine well.

**This** is the important bit. The remaining two-thirds of meringue have to be folded through the mixture. Dollop it in and, using your best exaggerated stirring movement, lightly fold the whites through the rich chocolate until the two mixtures are fully incorporated. Ladle the mixture into 6 serving mugs or glasses and leave in the fridge for at least 4 hours, or overnight.

- **When** ready to serve, top the mousses with a sprinkling of chopped hazelnuts. Serve up to your friends. Conversation, and possibly breathing, will stop as you remind yourself how good Nutella is.

# ETON MESS

The perfect beginners' dessert because there is almost no way you can go wrong with this recipe. The clue is in the title: 'mess'. Embrace the mess, and wow your friends on a hot summer's day by producing this dessert alongside some Pimms, or cider, or Special Brew, or White Lightning . . . Or whatever you are drinking; we're not judging you!

**SERVES 4**

½ jar of good-quality **strawberry jam**

300ml **double cream**

4 shop-bought **meringue** nests

8 fresh **strawberries**, roughly chopped (optional)

**Place** the jam and 3 tablespoons of water into a small saucepan over a low heat. Warm through until the mixture is well combined. You have just made an instant strawberry sauce. Leave to cool.

**Pour** the cream into a bowl and whisk. At this point, if anybody around you has an electric whisk then become their best friend. If not, then fear not, as the effort you are putting in will ensure guilt-free calorie consumption later on.

**Whisk** the double cream until it reaches the soft peak stage. This is when you pull up a bit of the cream and it almost holds itself up. Resist the temptation to over-whip.

**Now**, take one of the meringues in your hands and crush it directly over the whipped cream. It really doesn't matter how big, or small the pieces are that fall into the cream. Repeat with the remaining 3 meringues before gently folding the mixture together to incorporate the meringue pieces.

**Pour** a quarter of your now cooled strawberry sauce in with the cream, and fold lightly – it does not all have to be mixed in.

**Spoon** the mixture into individual glasses and pour any remaining strawberry sauce equally over the desserts. Top artistically with fresh strawberries (if using), flick on the telly and eat.

**Tip:** *You can make the component parts of this recipe the day before and put them in the fridge overnight. Try to assemble the mess as close to eating as possible.*

# MAKESHIFT APPLE TART

Very often, just the look of a dish makes us turn our backs on any thought of reproducing it ourselves, and the classically French tarte aux pommes is a case in point. You may have passed them in your local bakery or supermarket, glistening at you with the beautiful arrogance that only a Parisian can possess, almost daring you to attempt one just so you can fail. Well, here's the good news; they're incredibly easy to make, and here's how.

**SERVES 4**

Flour, for dusting

1 x 500g pack of ready-made chilled **puff pastry**

5 tbsp **apple sauce**

6 **apples** (Cox and Braeburn), peeled, cored and thinly sliced

3 tbsp **caster sugar**

2 tbsp cold **butter**, cut into cubes

2 tbsp smooth **apricot jam**

**Preheat** the oven to 180°C (gas mark 4).

**Dust** a clean surface with a little flour. Roll out your puff pastry block using a rolling pin or empty bottle until it is about ½ cm thick all over. What shape you end up with is not really important, as long as it fits in your oven and is of a consistent thickness. Place the pastry on a baking tray lined with parchment paper (transferring later will be very difficult).

**Spread** a generous amount of apple sauce over the pastry, ensuring that you leave a 2cm border around the edge.

**Scatter** your apple slices over the apple sauce. You want them to be roughly even in depth, and to maintain the 2cm border around the edge; a little order will ensure the most efficient covering of apples.

**Sprinkle** over the sugar and dot with the butter before baking in the oven for about 25 minutes. Once cooked, remove from the oven and leave to cool a little.

**Heat** up the apricot jam with 2 tablespoons of water in a small saucepan or in the microwave. Once the jam has melted into the water, brush the mixture all over the tart. This gives your creation that glistening patisserie finish.

**Serve** the tart either hot or cold and bask in your newfound baking confidence.

# SUMMER BERRY CRUMBLE

This is about as easy as a crumble can be – the fruit is frozen and the crumble topping uses ingredients straight out of your storecupboard, making this an impressive dessert to rustle up at short notice.

## SERVES 4

300g **plain flour**

150g cold **butter**, cut into cubes

170g **caster sugar**

1 kg **frozen berries**

Shop-bought **custard**, **ice cream** or pouring **cream**, to serve (optional)

**Preheat** the oven to 190°C (gas mark 5).

**Place** the flour and butter in a large bowl. Using your fingers and thumbs, rub the butter into the flour until you end up with a mixture that resembles breadcrumbs. Add the sugar (leaving back 1 tablespoon) and mix into the flour and butter with a fork.

**Tumble** your frozen berries straight into an ovenproof dish and sprinkle with the extra 1 tablespoon of sugar. Scatter over your crumble mixture and bake in the oven for 35 minutes, or until the top is golden and the fruit mixture is bubbling up the sides.

**Serve** your crumble with lashings of custard, ice cream or pouring cream.

**Tip:** *You don't need to stick with just frozen berries. Try experimenting with the frozen fruit at your local supermarket. Adding grated orange or lemon zest or mixed chopped nuts to the raw crumble mixture also adds some lip-smackingly good flavours.*

# FEEDING THE MASSES . . .

Just because you're a student doesn't mean you can't be civilised and throw a dinner party every now and then. Sure, your guests may have to eat from mismatched cutlery, and the last to arrive will have to drink their wine from mugs, but that's character, and right now, that's hip. Below are some of the events that we feel you may end up catering for, and our recommendations, for you to heed or ignore.

## STUDY GROUP

The time has come for the all-important final exams, and you have taken it upon yourself to make everyone else knuckle down with you by starting a study group However, you've just remembered that the only way you could convince your friends to give up their Sunday slobbery was by promising them a delicious dinner.

For a dish that will enhance your academic atmosphere, we suggest serving up one of the following:

- Prawns, Feta and Quinoa Salad (see page 114)

- Chorizo Chicken (see page 138)

- Gnocchi with Tomato Sauce and Ricotta (see page 128)

## BOYS OVER TO WATCH SPORT

Sometimes men just need to revert to their caveman status and huddle in a pack for a while in a place where we feel safe; a place away from the lipstick chat of womenfolk; a place where we can communicate in monosyllabic grunts, and where we're not judged for drinking lager straight from the can and that place is in front of the TV watching sport.

Whether you're chanting for your football team or marvelling at the body shapes throwing darts, you and your buddies need feeding. Look no further than the following recipe ideas to reinforce your manliness:

- Lamb Kebabs (see page 164)

- Soy-glazed Pork (see page 160)

- Chicken Pilaf (see pages 82–83)

## PARTY NIGHT OUT WITH THE GIRLS

Nails varnished, hair immaculate and killer heels ready to slip into: you are woman, and you are fierce.

The rest of the girls are arriving soon to put the finishing touches to their outfits. They're bringing the wine, but you need to feed them. When you need something light enough not to bloat, but substantial enough to keep you fuelled to the end of the night, try one of the following:

- Salmon Dinner in a Bag (see pages 132–133)

- Chicken Dinner in a Tray (see page 78)

- Sausage, Sweet Potato and Pepper Tray Bake (see page 144)

## LOVE IS IN THE AIR

You caught each other's eyes from afar, you shared a drunken snog, and now you're ready to up the ante with a home-cooked meal that you're hoping will convince them to stay the night.

You need food that exudes natural sexiness and maybe makes up for the cheesy Luther Vandross and Barry White in the background. Feed anybody the following menu and watch their heart slowly melt in front of you:

- Baked Camembert for Two (see page 131)

- Hearty Fish Pie (see pages 84–85)

- 'Mugged' Chocolate Hazelnut Mousse (see pages 192–193)

- Sweetcorn Fritters with Avocado Salsa (see page 54) – this is for the morning after. We're so very confident in our menu that we advise you to plan for the next morning.

## IN-LAWS TO BE

Your new and endlessly exciting relationship has been blossoming for a while now. However, the time has come to meet the in-laws, and you want to serve them something that, with every mouthful, reinforces your honourable intentions and shows off your home-making skills. Well, look no further than the following menu:

- *Starter*: Soda Bread (see page 33) served with smoked salmon on the side

- *Main*: Cottage Pie (see page 104)

- *Dessert*: Eton Mess (see page 194)

# INDEX

## A

all-American pancakes **174**

anchovies

  broccoli and anchovy spaghetti **42**

apple tart, makeshift **196**

Asian dressing **16**

asparagus **17**

avocados

  avocado salsa **54**

  guacamole **140**

## B

bacon

  bacon and lentil soup **73**

  bacon and pea spaghetti **44**

  chicken pilaf **82–83**

  easy chicken stew **80–81**

  pappardelle carbonara **46**

  Savoy cabbage and bacon **18**

baked beans

  posh beans on toast **63**

banana and chocolate loaf **185**

beans

  bean cassoulet **70**

  posh beans on toast **63**

beef

  cottage pie **104**

  good old burger 'n' sauce **168**

  Mamma Mia's lasagne **148**

  Momma's meatballs and spaghetti **86–87**

  multi-purpose mince **38–39**

  roast beef with Yorkshire puddings and gravy **98–99**

  spag bol **39**

  the ultimate beef stew **146–147**

berry crumble **198**

Black Forest pint-o-trifle **190**

blue cheese mushrooms on toast **113**

boiled egg **26**

bread

  soda bread **33**

  mushroom and herb filo rolls **106**

  see also toast

broccoli **17**

  broccoli and anchovy spaghetti **42**

  pork chop with easy gravy **94**

salmon dinner in a bag **132**

  tuna pasta bake **66**

bulgur wheat, chicken and **136**

burger 'n' sauce **168**

butter beans

  bean cassoulet **70**

buttercream **180**

butternut squash and goat's cheese risotto **112**

## C

cabbage **17, 18**

  Savoy cabbage and bacon **18**

  white cabbage coleslaw **18**

Caesar dressing **16**

cakes

  banana and chocolate loaf **185**

  chocolate crispy cakes **186**

  the ultimate vanilla cupcakes **180–181**

Camembert for two **131**

cannellini beans

  bean cassoulet **70**

caper dressing, Parmesan pork schnitzel with **92–93**

carb-loaded pesto pasta **64**

carbonara, pappardelle **46**

carrots **17, 20**

  bacon and lentil soup **73**

  carrot and swede mash **103**

  cottage pie **104**

  multi-purpose mince **38–39**

  roast vegetables **102**

  the ultimate beef stew **146–147**

cassoulet, bean **70**

cauliflower cheese **102**

celery **21**

cheese

  baked Camembert for two **131**

  butternut squash and goat's cheese risotto **112**

  cauliflower cheese **102**

  cheese sauce **31**

  cheesy easy omelette **49**

  chicken and bulgur wheat **136**

  fajita party **140–141**

  fancy blue cheese mushrooms on toast **113**

  gnocchi with tomato sauce and ricotta **128**

  mac 'n' cheese **90**

  Mamma Mia's lasagne **148**

Parmesan pork schnitzel with caper dressing **92–93**

prawn, feta and quinoa salad **114**

proper cheese on toast **62**

quesadillas **141**

tomato, mozzarella and basil pizza **170–171**

tuna pasta bake **66**

unbelievably easy ham and cheese pasty **124–125**

cherries

  Black Forest pint-o-trifle **190**

chicken

  chicken and bulgur wheat **136**

  chicken and ham toastie **52**

  chicken pilaf **82–83**

  chicken and sweet potato curry **158**

  chicken dinner on a tray **78**

  chorizo chicken **138**

  easy chicken stew **80–81**

  easy coronation chicken sandwiches **121**

  fajita party **140–141**

  my first chicken fricassee **48**

  piri-piri chicken **152**

  quesadillas **141**

  roast chicken and gravy **96–97**

  sticky honeyed chicken **157**

chickpeas

  chorizo chicken **138**

chillies

  broccoli and anchovy spaghetti **42**

  curried potatoes **72**

  guacamole **140**

  Indian lamb curry **166**

  piri-piri chicken **152**

  prawn, feta and quinoa salad **114**

  soy-glazed pork **160**

  sticky honeyed chicken **157**

chocolate

  banana and chocolate loaf **185**

  Black Forest pint-o-trifle **190**

  'mugged' chocolate hazelnut mousse **192–193**

  peanut butter and chocolate cookies **182**

  raspberry and white chocolate muffins **178**

  rocky road **188**

chopping boards **10**

chorizo sausage

  chorizo chicken **138**

sausage and red pepper rolls **118**
coconut milk
  chicken and sweet potato curry **158**
coleslaw, white cabbage **18**
cookies, peanut butter and chocolate **182**
corn on the cob, griddled **154**
coronation chicken sandwiches **121**
cottage pie **104**
courgettes
  tuna and courgette fritters **117**
cream
  Black Forest pint-o-trifle **190**
  Eton mess **194**
  fancy blue cheese mushrooms on toast **113**
  'mugged' chocolate hazelnut mousse **192–193**
  sloshed mussels **134**
crispy cakes, chocolate **186**
crumble, summer berry **198**
cucumber
  duck noodle stir-fry **56**
  a kind of 'pickled' cucumber salad **163**
  prawn, feta and quinoa salad **114**
Cup a Soup mushroom risotto **88–89**
cupcakes, the ultimate vanilla **180–181**
curries
  chicken and sweet potato curry **158**
  curried potatoes **72**
  easy coronation chicken sandwiches **121**
  Indian lamb curry **166**

D
digestive biscuits
  rocky road **188**
dinner party menus **200–201**
dishes, ovenproof **10**
dressings **16**
  Asian dressing **16**
  Caesar dressing **16**
  caper dressing **92–93**
  French dressing **16**
duck
  duck noodle stir-fry **56**

E
eggs **26–28**
  boiled egg **26**
  cheesy easy omelette **49**

eggs pipérade **50**
  fried egg **28**
  No. 42 all-purpose egg-fried rice **155**
  pappardelle carbonara **46**
  poached egg **28**
  scrambled egg **26**
  simple potato salad **47**
  Spanish omelette **110–111**
equipment **10–11**
Eton mess **194**

F
fajita party **140–141**
filo rolls, mushroom and herb **106**
fine beans **17**
fish
  broccoli and anchovy spaghetti **42**
  hearty fish pie **84–85**
  salmon dinner in a bag **132**
  teriyaki salmon **162**
  tuna and courgette fritters **117**
  tuna mayonnaise sandwiches **120**
  tuna pasta bake **66**
food poisoning **15**
French dressing **16**
fricassee
  my first chicken fricassee **48**
  pea and leek fricassé **95**
fried egg **28**
fritters
  sweetcorn fritters **54**
  tuna and courgette fritters **117**
fruit
  summer berry crumble **198**
frying pans **11**

G
garlic **20–21**
  chicken dinner on a tray **78**
  garlic mushrooms on toast **63**
  piri-piri chicken **152**
gnocchi **36–37**
  gnocchi with tomato sauce and ricotta **128**
goat's cheese
  butternut squash and goat's cheese risotto **112**
gravy **96–97, 98–99**
  easy gravy **94**
green beans **17**
  carb-loaded pesto pasta **64**
guacamole **140**

H
haddock
  hearty fish pie **84–85**
ham
  cheesy easy omelette **49**
  chicken and ham toastie **52**
  unbelievably easy ham and cheese pasty **124–125**
hazelnut mousse, 'mugged' chocolate **192–193**
hearty fish pie **84–85**
honeyed chicken **157**

I
Indian lamb curry **166**
Irish potato cakes **37**

K
kale
  chorizo chicken **138**
kebabs, lamb **164**
knives **10**

L
lamb
  Indian lamb curry **166**
  lamb kebabs **164**
lasagne **39**
  Mamma Mia's lasagne **148**
leeks
  chicken pilaf **82–83**
  hearty fish pie **84–85**
  pea and leek fricassee **95**
lemon
  salmon dinner in a bag **132**
lentils
  bacon and lentil soup **73**
  old-school sausages and lentils **74**

M
mac 'n' cheese **90**
makeshift apple tart **196**
Mamma Mia's lasagne **148**
mangetout **17**
marshmallows
  chocolate crispy cakes **186**
  rocky road **188**
mayonnaise
  easy coronation chicken sandwiches **121**
  good old burger 'n' sauce **168**
  prawn cocktail sandwiches **120**

simple potato salad **47**

tuna mayonnaise sandwiches **120**

white cabbage coleslaw **18**

measurements **8–9**

meatballs and spaghetti **86–87**

menus **200–201**

meringues

Eton mess **194**

mince **38–39**

Mamma Mia's lasagne **148**

Momma's meatballs and spaghetti **86–87**

mousse, 'mugged' chocolate hazelnut **192–193**

muffins, raspberry and white chocolate **178**

'mugged' chocolate hazelnut mousse **192–193**

mushrooms

Cup a Soup mushroom risotto **88–89**

fancy blue cheese mushrooms on toast **113**

garlic mushrooms on toast **63**

mushroom and herb filo rolls **106**

mussels, sloshed **134**

N

Nana's scones **176**

noodles

duck noodle stir-fry **56**

No. 42 all-purpose egg-fried rice **155**

nutrition **14**

nuts

mushroom and herb filo rolls **106**

O

old-school sausages and lentils **74**

omelettes

cheesy easy omelette **49**

Spanish omelette **110–111**

onions **20–21**

chicken dinner on a tray **78**

easy chicken stew **80–81**

eggs pipérade **50**

lamb kebabs **164**

piri-piri chicken **152**

roast vegetables **102**

salsa **141**

sausages, sweet potato and pepper tray bake **144**

Spanish omelette **110–111**

the ultimate beef stew **146–147**

ovenproof dishes **10**

P

pancakes **34**

all-American pancakes **174**

pancetta

bacon and lentil soup **73**

pappardelle carbonara **46**

Parmesan pork schnitzel with caper dressing **92–93**

parsnips

roast vegetables **102**

party menus **200–201**

pasta **22–23**

bacon and pea spaghetti **44**

broccoli and anchovy spaghetti **42**

carb-loaded pesto pasta **64**

mac 'n' cheese **90**

Mamma Mia's lasagne **148**

Momma's meatballs and spaghetti **86–87**

pappardelle carbonara **46**

sausage and tomato spaghetti **68**

spag bol **39**

tuna pasta bake **66**

pastries

mushroom and herb filo rolls **106**

sausage and red pepper rolls **118**

unbelievably easy ham and cheese pasty **124–125**

peanut butter and chocolate cookies **182**

peas **17**

bacon and pea spaghetti **44**

butternut squash and goat's cheese risotto **112**

cottage pie **104**

pea and leek fricassee **95**

peppers

chorizo chicken **138**

eggs pipérade **50**

prawn, feta and quinoa salad **114**

sausage and red pepper rolls **118**

sausages, sweet potato and pepper tray bake **144**

pesto pasta, carb-loaded **64**

'pickled' cucumber salad **163**

pies

cottage pie **104**

hearty fish pie **84–85**

*see also* pastries

pilaf, chicken **82–83**

piri-piri chicken **152**

pizza

tomato, mozzarella and basil **170–171**

planning **12–13**

poached egg **28**

pork

Parmesan pork schnitzel with caper dressing **92–93**

pork chop with easy gravy **94**

soy-glazed pork **160**

posh beans on toast **63**

potatoes **17, 19**

baked potatoes **19**

carb-loaded pesto pasta **64**

chicken dinner on a tray **78**

cottage pie **104**

curried potatoes **72**

easy chicken stew **80–81**

gnocchi **36–37**

hearty fish pie **84–85**

Irish potato cakes **37**

mashed potatoes **19**

roasted potatoes **19**

salmon dinner in a bag **132**

simple potato salad **47**

Spanish omelette **110–111**

wedges **19**

prawns

hearty fish pie **84–85**

prawn cocktail sandwiches **120**

prawn, feta and quinoa salad **114**

Q

quesadillas **141**

quinoa

prawn, feta and quinoa salad **114**

R

raisins

rocky road **188**

raspberry and white chocolate muffins **178**

rice **22**

butternut squash and goat's cheese risotto **112**

chicken pilaf **82–83**

Cup a Soup mushroom risotto **88–89**

No. 42 all-purpose egg-fried rice **155**

ricotta cheese

gnocchi with tomato sauce and ricotta **128**

risotto
  butternut squash and goat's cheese risotto **112**
  Cup a Soup mushroom risotto **88–89**
roast dinners
  roast beef with Yorkshire puddings and gravy **98–99**
  roast chicken and gravy **96–97**
  roast vegetables **102**
rocky road **188**

S
safety **15**
sage and onion stuffing
  pork chop with easy gravy **94**
salads
  a kind of 'pickled' cucumber salad **163**
  prawn, feta and quinoa salad **114**
  simple potato salad **47**
  white cabbage coleslaw **18**
  see also dressings
salmon
  salmon dinner in a bag **132**
  teriyaki salmon **162**
salsa **141**
  avocado salsa **54**
sandwiches **120–121**
  easy coronation chicken **121**
  prawn cocktail **120**
  tuna mayonnaise **120**
saucepans **11**
sauces
  cheese sauce **31**
  easy gravy **94**
  good old burger 'n' sauce **168**
  gravy **96–97, 98–99**
  simple tomato sauce **29**
  white sauce **30–31**
sausages
  chorizo chicken **138**
  old-school sausages and lentils **74**
  sausage and red pepper rolls **118**
  sausage and tomato spaghetti **68**
  sausages with sweet potato and pepper tray bake **144**
Savoy cabbage **17**
  Savoy cabbage and bacon **18**
scones, Nana's **176**
scrambled egg **26**
sherry

roast chicken and gravy **96–97**
shopping **12–13**
sloshed mussels **134**
smoked haddock
  hearty fish pie **84–85**
soda bread **33**
soup, bacon and lentil **73**
soured cream
  fajita party **140–141**
soy sauce
  soy-glazed pork **160**
  teriyaki salmon **162**
spaghetti
  bacon and pea spaghetti **44**
  broccoli and anchovy spaghetti **42**
  carb-loaded pesto pasta **64**
  Momma's meatballs and spaghetti **86–87**
  sausage and tomato spaghetti **68**
  spag bol **39**
Spanish omelette **110–111**
spinach **18**
  chicken and sweet potato curry **158**
  chicken dinner on a tray **78**
  curried potatoes **72**
squash
  butternut squash and goat's cheese risotto **112**
stews
  bean cassoulet **70**
  easy chicken stew **80–81**
  the ultimate beef stew **146–147**
sticky honeyed chicken **157**
stir-fry, duck noodle **56**
strawberries
  Eton mess **194**
summer berry crumble **198**
swede
  carrot and swede mash **103**
sweet potatoes **19**
  chicken and sweet potato curry **158**
  sausages, sweet potato and pepper tray bake **144**
sweetcorn fritters **54**

T
tart, makeshift apple **196**
teriyaki salmon **162**
toast
  chicken and ham toastie **52**
  fancy blue cheese mushrooms on toast **113**

garlic mushrooms on toast **63**
posh beans on toast **63**
proper cheese on toast **62**
tomatoes on toast **60**
tomatoes
  avocado salsa **54**
  bean cassoulet **70**
  chicken dinner on a tray **78**
  chorizo chicken **138**
  easy chicken stew **80–81**
  eggs pipérade **50**
  gnocchi with tomato sauce and ricotta **128**
  good old burger 'n' sauce **168**
  Indian lamb curry **166**
  mac 'n' cheese **90**
  Momma's meatballs and spaghetti **86–87**
  multi-purpose mince **38–39**
  old-school sausages and lentils **74**
  salsa **141**
  sausage and tomato spaghetti **68**
  simple tomato sauce **29**
  tomato, mozzarella and basil pizza **170–171**
  tomatoes on toast **60**
  the ultimate beef stew **146–147**
tortillas **121**
  fajita party **140–141**
  quesadillas **141**
trifles
  Black Forest pint-o-trifle **190**
tuna
  tuna and courgette fritters **117**
  tuna mayonnaise sandwiches **120**
  tuna pasta bake **66**

V
vegetables **17–21**
  roast vegetables **102**

W
white sauce **30–31**
wine
  roast chicken and gravy **96–97**
  sloshed mussels **134**
wooden chopping boards **10**

Y
Yorkshire puddings **98–99**

# Get your meal seen by MILLIONS on Student Beans.com

Yep, you heard right MILLIONS!

So how about it? Send us a pic of the dish you've just made from this book, and we'll put it in our hall of fame along with the date it was made, your name(s) and university.

... and you could be famous like this guy

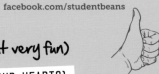

Feel free to be in the photo, not be in the photo, put your Lego men in the photo, do what the hell you like with the photo (though try to get the dish in there somewhere).

→ send your entries to hello@studentbeans.com

studentbeans.com is the **BIGGEST** student site in the UK, specialising in freebies, jobs and special discounts just for students.

We also create loads of articles designed to be incredibly useful to students, for example:

8 UNFORGIVABLE CV MISTAKES

6 WORST MONEY WASTING DANGER ZONES!!!

10 SIMPLE WAYS TO BEAT PROCRASTINATION

Or incredibly intriguing

UNIVERSITY SEX LEAGUE   THE ULTIMATE GUIDE TO NAPPING

99 THINGS TO DO BEFORE YOU LEAVE UNIVERSITY

Like us on Facebook
facebook.com/studentbeans

Or just plain silly (but very fun)

28 KIDS WHO FAIL AT DRAWING (BUT STEAL OUR HEARTS)

24 INAPPROPRIATE FANCY-DRESS COSTUMES FOR KIDS

WHAT CRAZY NATIONAL DAY FALLS ON YOUR BIRTHDAY?

@studentbeans

It's no wonder that we have over **2 MILLION** visits each month from students

# ACKNOWLEDGEMENTS

This book would not have been possible without the support of many people.

The biggest thanks of all go to our immediate families. Rob's wife Hannah and son Theo, for giving him the motivation, time and support to work on the book, and his mum, dad and brother for always being there (in the kitchen). Michael's wife Stephanie, son Toby and daughter Mia, for their encouragement, patience and love. We would also like to thank our parents, Bernard and Diana, and siblings Simon, Hannah and Ben, for their unwavering support in setting up and establishing studentbeans.com.

This book would never have come about without the passion and dedication of our agent Jonathan Conway. Thank you also to the excellent team at Orion. In particular, Amanda Harris for commissioning the book; Kate Wanwimolruk, our editor, for her energy and guidance, and Abi Hartshorne and Lucie Stericker for their thoughtful design and creativity.

Thank you to Andrew Hayes-Watkins who took all the mouth-watering photographs and to Raf Szybowski and Leonie Sooke for their help in making the food look so spectacular.

A huge thanks to the wonderful studentbeans.com team, in particular Oliver Brann for his skilful editorial direction and badassness and Barrie Smith for his inspiration and art direction. Thank you to Daniel Nabarro who has always been there to support us and share his wisdom.

We would also like to thank Rachel Davies of Rachel's Kitchen for helping to create the excellent prequel to this book, Fraser Doughty for sharing his entrepreneurial lessons, The Prince's Trust for their exceptional mentoring when we were starting out and David Taylor, The Naked Leader, for his impetus to create this book. Finally, we would like to thank our housemates when we were at university, who made cooking and life in the kitchen so memorable – in Birmingham: Naomi, Claire, Caz, Helen and Becky; and in Nottingham: Katie, Richard, Romy and Marcus.

— *Michael and James Eder, founders of studentbeans.com*

First published in Great Britain in 2013

by Weidenfeld & Nicolson, an imprint of Orion Publishing Group Ltd

Orion House, 5 Upper St Martin's Lane, London WC2H 9EA

an Hachette UK company

10 9 8 7 6 5 4 3 2 1

A CIP catalogue record for this book is available from the British Library.

ISBN: 978-0-297-86997-9

Words and recipes: Rob Allison

Food director's assistant: Leonie Sooke

Cover and inside photography: Andrew Hayes-Watkins

Designer and art director: Abi Hartshorne

Project editor: Kate Wanwimolruk

Copy-editor: Abi Waters

Proofreader: Holly Kyte

Indexer: Hilary Bird

**Note:** All eggs are medium-sized and butter unsalted, unless otherwise stated.

Printed and bound in Italy

The Orion Publishing Group's policy is to use papers that are natural, renewable and recyclable products and made from wood grown in sustainable forests. The logging and manufacturing processes are expected to conform to the environmental regulations of the country of origin.

www.orionbooks.co.uk